Literacy Coaching: The Essentials

Katherine Casey

Foreword by Anthony J. Alvarado

HEINEMANN
PORTSMOUTH, NH

Heinemann
A division of Reed Elsevier Inc.
361 Hanover Street
Portsmouth, NH 03801–3912
www.heinemann.com

Offices and agents throughout the world

Library of Congress Cataloging-in-Publication Data
Casey, Katherine.
  Literacy coaching : the essentials / Katherine Casey ; foreword by Anthony J. Alvarado.
      p. cm.
  Includes bibliographical references and index.
  ISBN 0-325-00941-4 (alk. paper)
  1. Language arts teachers—Training of—United States. 2. Literacy—Study and teaching—United States. I. Title.

LB1576.C31796 2006
428.4'071—dc22   2006008252

Editor: Harvey Daniels
Production: Patricia Adams
Typesetter: SPi
Cover design: Judith Arisman
Cover photography: Rey Moreno
Manufacturing: Steve Bernier

Printed in the United States of America on acid-free paper
10 09 08 07 06   EB   2 3 4 5

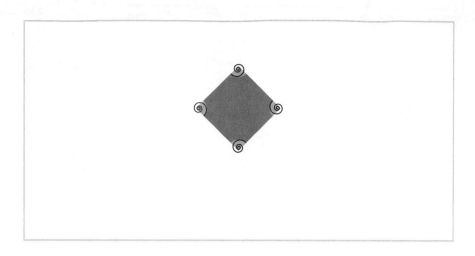

For my principal,
Anna Marie Carrillo

Contents

Foreword

"Good" books in our field are books that tend to achieve their authors' purposes, and while these may be reasonably narrow, there is usually an exposition of subject matter that is persuasive and enlightening, clear, and comprehensive. Readers are able to more effectively apply the suggestions, examples, tools, and insights of the text.

Ideally, however, writers try to write "extraordinary" books, which can synthesize disparate phenomena, capture a broader set of values, are useful to a wider professional community and, ultimately, make an original contribution to the field. Extraordinary books are layered with meaning; can and should be revisited because they continue to impart knowledge and guide reflection; generate understanding and support to professionals with varying degrees of expertise; seamlessly join theory and practice; and, perhaps most importantly, teach and model how to solve problems and how to use evidence to grow, learn, make better decisions, and improve results. Extraordinary books are not easy, but reward vigorous study handsomely. They keep purpose squarely at the center of intellectual activity and do not let the reader off the hook with superficial or slovenly interpretations. Katherine Casey has written an extraordinary book.

Katherine Casey shows aspiring, new, and experienced coaches how to think about their work, how to organize it, how to do it, and how to improve it. She understands that coaches, like teachers, need to see how the problems of practice are identified and addressed. Coaches will appreciate the level of detail that she provides; the examples of communication both in dialogue and in written form; the guidance provided in observing, note taking, explicating structures of professional development; and the asking of questions that keep the work of coaches on track.

This book addresses what is perhaps the central instructional problem in America today. How do we teach all children to use language powerfully and effectively in order to think intelligently about the world and how they relate to it? So, while the text teaches how to coach, the substance of this coaching is literacy and this book is a rich source of literacy content and practice.

Katherine understands that professional development cannot avoid the tricky and complex task of dealing with individuals' deep feelings about who they are, what they know, and the vulnerabilities inherent in learning and making their work public. She devotes an entire chapter to working successfully with the principal, a subject so often ignored, yet key to the success of literacy coaches. Every coaching example contains strategies for successfully engaging individuals, stressing both the knowledge/skill and the human dimension.

This book does not create the usual content silos around important topics—assessments, standards, data-driven decision making, technology, and so on—which teachers and coaches then find impossible to effectively incorporate into their pedagogy. The text achieves something that is rare in professional development books. It demonstrates how to integrate core instructional elements into successful practice.

A careful reader of this book will have made a professional colleague of the author. When planning, coaching, or debriefing, readers will continually ask, What would Katherine say? What is the evidence for my judgment? If teachers could not implement a strategy, what did I fail to achieve with them? Katherine becomes the reader's professional conscience, which both expects a professional standard of performance and constantly supports its attainment.

While this book is addressed to literacy coaches, it is inherently about the improvement of instruction and is therefore a rich resource for teachers, principals, and district office leadership. Coaches are part of an educational organization whose culture either supports and enhances their efforts or works at cross purposes to it. This book should become a central text for study at the classroom, school, and district level.

A book of this caliber could only have been written by an exceptional professional. Having had the privilege of witnessing, firsthand, Katherine Casey's remarkable work as a teacher and coach, it is clear why the book is as good as it is and why it will be of extraordinary service to practitioners everywhere.

Anthony J. Alvarado

Acknowledgments

Echoing throughout this book are the voices of many people who taught me along the way. How grateful I am that I began my teaching career at PS 116, led by an exceptional educator, Anna Marie Carrillo, who provided me with every imaginable support and learning opportunity as I figured out how to be a teacher. Thank you, Anna Marie, and thank you to the PS 116 staff and to my students and their families.

I learned to coach from the examples set by a handful of powerful educators who worked alongside me in my classroom at PS 116. My first literacy coach, Leslie Zackman, exemplifies excellence in teaching and coaching. Lucy West not only taught me how to teach mathematics and how to coach, but also transformed my beliefs about education by showing me how to build communities of learners. Donna Santman's incredibly smart and challenging teaching inspired me to embrace literacy. Gaby Layden made both reading and writing workshop come alive in my classroom. I thank each of you for what and how you taught me.

I am thankful that I taught in New York City's District 2 under the visionary leadership of Tony Alvarado and Elaine Fink. I am doubly lucky that I had the opportunity to work with Tony in San Diego City Schools and Elaine in the Educational Leadership Development Academy at the University of San Diego. My knowledge and skill as a teacher, coach, and educational leader are direct outcomes of their intense focus on high-quality professional development.

Educators across the country have welcomed me into their classrooms, schools, and literacy departments. I am inspired by their generosity and by their willingness to engage in the hard work of transforming teaching and learning. A big thank-you to the educators I worked with in San Diego City Schools, especially Debbie Beldock, Ann Van Sickle, Melinda Martin, Carol

Osborne, Lyn Reggett, Jolie Pickett, Bernie Nguyen, Robin Hodgkinson, Stacy Spector, Laura Brown, Barbra Balser, Ginger Blackmon, Vincent Riveroll, and Shannon Maul. And a thank-you to the educators in the Kansas City, Missouri, School District; the Norwalk La Mirada Unified School District; Highline Public Schools; Marysville Public Schools; and the Nooksack Valley School District.

I must thank Lisa Young, the first teacher I ever coached in a gradual-release coaching cycle, for her courage and grace under pressure. You let me figure out how to become a side-by-side coach during our days together.

Kate Montgomery sent me emails periodically, prodding me to consider writing a book with Heinemann, until I just could not procrastinate a moment longer. Thank you, Kate, for helping find my writer's voice. When I learned that Smokey Daniels, the author of many professional texts that profoundly shaped my teaching, would be my editor, I couldn't believe my good fortune. Smokey, I am grateful for your enthusiasm, witty margin notes, and expert guidance throughout the writing process.

This book would not have been written without the persistent encouragement of my dear friends Ginny Lockwood Zisa and Katherine Bescherer Berger, who cheered me along with emails, phone calls, and love from across the country; and Leslie Barnes and Wilma Kozai, my local cheering squad. Knowing I couldn't let you down kept me writing when I wanted to call it quits.

My parents and first teachers, Joe and Kay Casey, instilled in me their belief in the power an outstanding education has to transform lives. Though my mother is proud enough for both of them, I wish my father were alive to read this book, since how he lived his life inspires me and I miss him every day. I am grateful to my sister, Liz Anne, and brothers Mark and Michael for their enthusiastic support of my commitment to education.

And my sweet husband, Joel, for the confidence and trust you have in my abilities, for the utter belief in our work as educators, and for knowing, well before I did, that we are happier and more powerful together than we are apart, I thank you forever.

Part I   What Coaches Do

 The Goals of This Book

Literacy coaching offers great promise as a field. In our roles as coaches, we are poised to actually craft ongoing and supportive learning opportunities for teachers and students alike. We can help put an end to sending teachers to generic workshops that do not address our specific contexts, our students, our concerns and needs. We can help develop and nurture relationships with our colleagues that focus on problem solving how to meet the needs of our students, and can spend time together in classrooms, not isolated and alone, figuring out what needs to happen for our students and for us to increase student achievement. What an exciting and daunting challenge, especially in a profession accustomed to wide instructional and philosophical pendulum swings, and less-than-effective professional development, and sagging under the weight of high-stakes testing.

Part I offers ideas and strategies that will help you navigate your way on your coaching journey. Chapter 1 offers guidance for how to get started as a literacy coach, from establishing relationships in a school, to gathering the necessary supplies, to adjustments you may need to make if you are transitioning from a teacher to a literacy coach.

Literacy coaching is an evolving field with numerous definitions of what it means to be a literacy coach, so Chapter 2 addresses the specifics of what a literacy coach needs to know and be able to do. Though I am making the assumption that you already know a lot about literacy, at the end of the book I offer an annotated bibliography of resources that I turn to for additional knowledge and support.

Because principal leadership is essential in the improvement of instruction, establishing a strong relationship with your principal is essential to effective literacy coaching. Chapter 3 is devoted to how you and the principal can establish an environment conducive to supporting professional growth.

Chapter 4 shows you how to begin the work of determining teachers' strengths and needs using a variety of methods, including conversations with teachers and classroom observations, so that you can develop a plan for how to provide the necessary support.

Me, a Coach?

"You do *what* for a living? What do you mean you're a *literacy coach*?" I struggle to answer those questions and help people understand what I do every day. For the past five years, I've worked in a variety of districts as a reading and writing consultant. I'm hired by universities, districts, and schools to lead professional development sessions of all sizes. In three urban school districts I regularly teach administrators, coaches, and teachers about literacy—everything from how students learn to read and write, to what students need for their learning, to instructional best practices, to what leaders need to know and be able to do to help teachers increase student achievement. I coach teachers in their classrooms by demonstrating lessons, working alongside them as they teach, and problem-solving with them to better meet the needs of their students.

This is not exactly what I set out to do when I became an elementary school teacher in New York City Public Schools in the early 1990s. I was the teacher who insisted I'd never leave the classroom, would never feel comfortable teaching reading and writing (mathematics was my strength), and would never leave my school and district. As soon as I started teaching, my principal, Anna Marie Carrillo, provided me with myriad professional development opportunities, from attending conferences and institutes to school site workshops. Her outstanding staff developers worked alongside me in my classroom, helping my students to learn and me to teach. I grew up in a district and school that encouraged classroom observations, so I became accustomed to teaching as people watched and often participated in lessons. Over time I found myself welcoming teachers into my classroom and became a teacher leader myself, working alongside colleagues in their classrooms. Other districts invited me to work with their teachers and, with increasing knowledge and skill, I became passionate about literacy coaching.

I find I am not alone in my role as a coach—or in my struggle to define my job. Literacy coaching is quickly becoming the number-one staff development model (Manzo 2005). The concept of the literacy coach emerged in the 1920s (Hall 2004), and, throughout the decades since, various methods of coaching have evolved—technical coaching, collegial coaching (Dantonio 2001), cognitive coaching (Costa and Garmston 2002), peer coaching (Joyce and Showers 2002), content-focused coaching (West and Staub 2003), and many others (Greene 2004). The variety of coaching methods reveals educators' determination to devise ways to respectfully and effectively support teachers in the improvement of instruction while navigating the inevitable unsteadiness accompanying change and the probable tensions that arise when teachers are asked to examine their instructional practices.

We are in the midst of a literacy coaching boom (Hatch 2003) and literacy coaching is evolving, growing, and unstable. Our nation is embarking on an unprecedented and high-stakes effort to raise student achievement by improving teaching and learning for all students. Faced with the daunting task of meeting all students' needs, school districts are recognizing that past professional development practices—comprised largely of university coursework, stand-alone workshops, or conferences—cannot provide all the support teachers need. "The rapid proliferation of reading coaches is one of the responses to increased attention to reading achievement and the achievement gap in the United States," the International Reading Association (IRA 2004) explains. Adding to the instability of literacy coaching is the wide variability in job descriptions, skill level, qualifications, and training of coaches (IRA 2004).

The basic role of the literacy coach has evolved as a way to provide job-embedded, context-specific, ongoing support to teachers and students. Literacy coaches and teachers work together to improve instructional practice in order to raise student achievement. Literacy coaches:

- help design and facilitate professional development sessions tailored to address issues facing teachers and students;
- work alongside teachers in classrooms, demonstrating instructional strategies and guiding teachers as they try on the strategies;
- evaluate students' literacy needs and collaborate with teachers to design instruction to meet those needs;
- provide teachers with ongoing opportunities to learn from and with each other.

Literacy coaching involves creating and sustaining relationships and, like any relationship, it is dynamic. Coaches work to establish trust, open lines of communication, and cultivate an atmosphere of collegial collaboration and problem solving with their teachers. Together with their teachers, literacy coaches grapple with how to observe, discuss, examine, and improve instructional practice that historically has occurred behind closed doors. Coaches continually work to improve their teaching of both students and adults. Just because one is an effective teacher of children does not mean one is an effective teacher of adults.

Literacy coaching also involves skillfully working within a district context. In some school districts, literacy coaching is teacher centered, requested by the teacher and focused on the teacher's agenda. In other school districts, literacy coaching is guided by school administrators, or program or grant requirements. Teachers are assigned coaches and are instructed to work on topics suggested by the district or principal. Coaching is considered a reform strategy and coaches are now mandated as part of the professional development requirements for Reading First, the early literacy component of No Child Left Behind Act (NCLB), signed into law by President George W. Bush in 2002. Developing trusting relationships is essential to the literacy coach's success (Lyons and Pinnell 2001; Robb 2000; Buly, Coskie, Robinson, and Egawa 2005). And establishing trust within today's often mandated relationships requires strong interpersonal skills, indeed. Depending on the district or school culture, the coach-teacher relationship can vary from almost sacred and largely private to quite public.

While the literacy coaching boom is new, we do have professional standards for middle and high school literacy coaches published by the International Reading Association and created in collaboration with a coalition of key professional organizations. Elementary school coaches, I encourage you to examine the standards, too, since what I talk about in this book upholds these standards: skillful collaborators, skillful job-embedded coaches, skillful evaluators of literacy needs, and skillful instructional strategists (IRA 2006).

What Type of Literacy Coach Are You?

Most likely, you're reading this book because you're a literacy coach, or you're a principal working with a coach, or maybe you're thinking about being a literacy coach.

If you are a literacy coach, let's start by answering the question: *What type of literacy coach are you?*

Because literacy coaching is an evolving aspect of American education and because the roles and responsibilities of literacy coaches vary widely across the country (Hall 2004), we do not have a uniform definition of literacy coaching. You may be one of a number of literacy coaches in your district who meet regularly for professional development focused on how to coach; to attend professional development sessions to "bring back" to schools; or to problem-solve coaching situations. Or you may rarely interact with other coaches. You may report to a central office or district supervisor or whoever runs the coaching program, or your principal may be your only supervisor. You may be assigned to a school at the principal's request or at the district's discretion or because coaching is part of a grant, such as Reading First. You may be a literacy coach because you were selected by teachers or administrators within your school to become a coach, perhaps transitioning from a reading specialist position. Depending on where you work, you may be called a literacy coach, academic coach, peer coach, staff developer, reading coach, mentor teacher, teacher educator, reading specialist coach, advisor/mentor, change coach, content coach, or, perhaps, something else.

For the sake of clarity, I will use the following terms to describe different types of literacy coaches.

School-Based Coach

If you are a school-based coach, you probably work full time or maybe half-day as a coach at one school for one principal. You may work with the entire staff, with specific departments or grade levels, with teachers using a particular curriculum, or with all the above.

Teacher Leader

If you are a teacher leader, you are a classroom teacher who teaches students and also coaches colleagues periodically throughout the week.

District Coach

If you are a district coach, you work full time for one district, and you are responsible for multiple schools within your district. Like a school-based coach, you may work with entire staffs, or with specific departments or grade levels, or with teachers using a particular curriculum, or with all the above. Unlike a school-based coach, you work with more than one principal and staff, requiring that you get to know a number of school communities. You may also report to a district supervisor, who guides and holds you accountable for your coaching work. You may conduct districtwide professional development sessions for teachers and you may also be responsible for providing professional development for school-based coaches or teacher leaders.

Consultant

If you are a consultant, you work periodically with schools in a number of districts. You may work at the school level with groups of teachers and you may conduct districtwide professional development sessions for teachers or literacy coaches, or you may do both.

The type of literacy coach you are shapes much of how you do your coaching work—how you schedule your time with teachers, what you work on with teachers, what you expect are the outcomes of your coaching work with teachers, and how you begin working in a school.

 ## Help! My Principal Just Made Me a Coach!

Because the coaching profession is rapidly evolving and expanding, you may find that your principal decided you should be a coach, seemingly overnight your roles and responsibilities have changed. Perhaps you are worried that people are questioning your credibility, wondering whether you've crossed the line to administrator, or thinking someone else should have been made coach instead of you. Certainly you are the topic of conversation among your peers, who are curious about how your coaching status is going to affect them in the classroom and their relationship with you outside the classroom. But remember that all the chatter is a normal response to any change that occurs in your school. Trust that as your coaching work begins to take shape, your anxiety and theirs will begin to subside. Until then, here's some advice.

- ◆ Try to refrain from hypothesizing with your teachers about what your role is going to be until you've had opportunities to define and discuss your role with your principal. Teachers will want to know with whom you'll work and why. Some principals encourage teachers to ask for coaching, while other principals want to be involved in the decision-making process, perhaps focusing your work within certain grade levels. Check with your principal about how you will decide with whom you'll work.

◆ Some teachers may equate coaching with an administrative, and therefore evaluative, position. You may have to repeatedly remind teachers that you are not their evaluator. Remind your principal to help send this important message, too.

◆ Expect colleagues to question your credibility. They should, especially if you haven't had coaching experience. You may be coaching people with more years of teaching experience, degrees, or credentials, or you may find yourself on unfamiliar grade levels. Establishing credibility will happen as your work with students and teachers begins to take hold. One of my colleagues didn't stop reminding me, "I've been teaching longer than you've been alive," until we figured out successful ways to support her English Learners.

◆ Recognize that your relationship with *everyone* in the school will undergo changes, which can be painful as well as joyous.
  • Your relationship with your principal will shift from teacher-principal to coach-principal (more on that in Chapter 3).
  • If you are personal friends with teachers at your school, you'll need to establish new boundaries about what you talk about, and that may feel awkward. Confidentiality and trust are vital to a coaching relationship. Though you may be tempted to share with your teacher friends what happens in another teacher's classroom or in a conversation with a colleague or administrator, you simply must not.
  • People will treat you differently and that takes some adjustment. One Friday afternoon I remember walking into Happy Hour a bit late. As I approached the table of colleagues and teacher friends, the group paused and then changed the subject. I later learned the group had been talking about the principal—which we often did—and worried that I would tell the principal what they had been discussing. I felt the sting of being in no man's land—no longer a teacher and not an administrator. But not all the changes are painful. A few weeks after the Happy Hour incident, a teacher came running up to me in the hallway, overjoyed to share a breakthrough with a challenging student our coaching relationship had caused. You, too, will be instrumental in bringing about exciting changes for students and teachers.

- Try to take comfort in what you do know about teaching and learning, since you can expect to be overwhelmed by how much you don't know. Every time I coach a teacher, I hear nagging whispers of self-doubt, once voiced in a staff meeting by a frustrated colleague, who shouted, "Who made *her* coach?" And every time I coach, I say to myself, "Focus on what the students need, focus on what the teacher needs, remember what you know about good teaching."

- Building trust is going to take time and careful steps on your part. Begin to get to know teachers by being visible and friendly where teachers gather informally such as the office, halls, and lunch area. Ask about the photos of family or friends teachers display, about upcoming weekend plans, how they spent the summer, about whatever helps you begin to establish a warm rapport. My schedule binder is covered with artifacts from my life—photos of family, a postcard from my vacation, an inspirational quote, a silly cartoon—and serves as a conversation starter. Compliment teachers on their student work displays or classroom environments. Listen for instructional materials teachers say they need, like terrific texts for read-aloud, and lend materials you may have.

- Remain open-minded to the possibilities that coaching relationships bring. Though the transition from classroom teacher to coach may hit rough patches, the rewards are remarkable when coach and teacher work together to provide students with the highest-quality education.

 ## How to Begin Working in a School

Information, more information, and even more information is what you need as you begin your work as a coach. The more you know about the context in which you are coaching, the better. If you are now a coach in a school where you taught, you may think you know enough about your school, but you probably don't have the information you need to inform your coaching work.

I found this entry I wrote in my writer's notebook two months after becoming a teacher leader in my school.

On which planet have I landed?!? I thought I knew my school inside and out . . . and I did, from my perspective as a fifth-grade teacher. I knew my students and their parents. I knew the fourth-grade teachers since I looped my students from fourth to fifth grade. I'm friends with lots of my colleagues; we eat lunch together every day and socialize outside of school. I had some practice working with my colleagues as grade leader and participated in every committee you can imagine! But I realize, now that I've started coaching, that I don't really know my colleagues as teachers and learners. Prior to this year, I hadn't spent time watching all of my colleagues teach, looking at their students' strengths and needs, and examining how my colleagues learn. I didn't have much of an idea of what the consistency of teaching and learning looked like for all students from my principal's perspective. I'm stunned by how much I don't know about my school, and I've spent the majority of my waking hours in this school building for the past five years. How is that possible?

Reading this entry brought back feelings of bewilderment that plagued me as I began my work as a teacher leader. I felt so unsteady on my nearly vertical learning curve, in part because I did not know what I did not know. When my principal asked me if I had any questions, I didn't even know what questions to ask and I didn't know the information I needed to gather.

Research the District and School Using the Internet

Now I gather information whenever I begin work with schools. The Internet puts information about schools, districts, and state departments of education just a few clicks away. If you "grew up" in your district, meaning you were a teacher in the district before becoming a coach, researching your district and school in this way may seem unnecessary. Just try it! You may discover new information that proves quite useful in your coaching work.

I recently began working with an elementary school in an urban school system in Southern California. Prior to my first meeting with school leaders, I used the Internet to gather information about the school district and the school. I Googled the school and found a link to the district website, which included a list of schools and information about each school. The elementary school's page included a link to the school report card and to a school fact sheet, both of which provided me with a great deal of information, which I compiled into a School Research Form (Figure 1–1). I downloaded both the school report card and the school fact sheet into a folder on my computer. I also printed a copy of both and put them into a binder labeled with the school's name.

After perusing state, district, and school websites, I reviewed the information on the School Research Form and started to build a picture of the

School *So. Cal. Elementary School*		
Questions	**Information**	**Resource**
Student population	670 students, K–5 18 (2.7%) African American 4 (0.6%) American Indian or Alaska Native 16 (2.4%) Asian 16 (2.4%) Filipino 585 (87.3%) Hispanic or Latino 2 (0.3%) Pacific Islander 29 (4.3%) White (not Hispanic) 0 (0.0%) Multiple or no response 39% English Learners ("Most of the 261 students at our school whose native language is not English speak Spanish at home") 79% low-income students	School accountability report card on district website
Mission statement	Our Elementary School serves the needs of the general education population as well as those of over 50 severely handicapped students. We believe that all students can learn and show progress despite the variety of challenges they may face. Our Elementary School strives to have all general education students read successfully by the age of nine. Our mission statement is "To Read Is To Succeed." Our Elementary School is committed to helping all students with severe handicaps to reach their individual learning plan goals.	School accountability report card on district website
Assessment requirements	• California Standards Test (CST) in English (grades 2–11) and Math (grades 2–11) • Science Standards Test (grades 5, 9, 10, and 11) • History and Social Science Standards Test (grades 8, 10, and 11) • CAT-6, a norm-referenced test, tests reading, language, and mathematics (grades 2–11), spelling (grades 2–8), and science (grades 9–11) • California Alternate Performance Assessment (CAPA) for students with "significant	School accountability report card on district website *Continues*

FIG. 1–1 School Research Form

Questions	Information	Resource
	cognitive disabilities who are unable to take the CST" (grades 2–11) • RIT–A local assessment, the Achievement Level Test of the Northwest Evaluation Association, tests reading, writing, and mathematics (grades 3–5)	
Released sample test items	Released CST questions are available on the California department of education website—all test grades and all tested subjects	www.cde.ca.gov
Achievement data	Percent of students achieving at proficient or advanced (meeting or exceeding the state standards) English Language Arts—20% of all students (31% of African Americans, 55% of Filipino, 19% of Hispanic or Latino, 35% of white students) Mathematics—33% of all students (31% of African American, 64% of Filipino, 31% Hispanic or Latino, 41% of white students) Science—7%	School accountability report card on district website
Annual yearly progress (AYP)	No—Not all AYP targets were met; specifically, targets for English Learners were not met	School accountability report card on district website
District/state standards	English Arts Standards (grades K–12) include: Reading Writing Listening and Speaking Mathematics Standards (grades K–12) History–Social Science Standards (grades K–12) Science Standards (grades K–12) Physical Education Standards (grades K–12) Visual and Performing Arts Standards (grades pre-K–12) English Language Development Standards (grades K–12)	District website District website State website State website State website State website State website
Curriculum materials	Doesn't say which ones on district or school website. Need to ask principal.	

FIG. 1–1 Cont.

elementary school. I learned that the majority of students, over 87 percent of the student population, are Hispanic or Latino. According to the school fact sheet, 264 (39 percent) of the students are English Learners. I noticed that the English Language Learner subgroup did not make Annual Yearly Progress (AYP) targets, so I expected that my literacy work with teachers would need to include ample attention paid to supports and strategies for English Language Learners.

Become Familiar with State, Local, and School-Based Standards and Assessments

I downloaded copies of all of the state standards into a computer folder labeled CA Standards—not just the English Language Arts standards, since I know that literacy happens across the content areas, and I planned to explicitly show teachers how to support literacy development across the content areas. While locating the standards on the state website, I noticed a link to released California Standards Test items, which I downloaded into a folder labeled CA Test Items so that I could become familiar with the format and content of the California Standards Test. Though the school website said that the elementary school uses state-approved curriculum materials, it did not specify which curriculum materials teachers currently use. As I reviewed the information, I started a list of questions (Figure 1–2) to ask and topics to discuss during my initial meeting with the principal.

If your school or district does not have an abundance of information available on a website, inquire at the school or district office. Or use the

So. Cal. Elementary School
Questions:
• Do you use a particular curriculum or textbook series?   • I noticed that 39 percent of your students are English Language Learners. What strategies do teachers currently use to support English Learners? Can we talk about how my coaching work can help support teachers as they support English Learners?   • In addition to the state and district tests, what types of assessments do your teachers use to inform their instructional decisions?

FIG. 1–2 Questions for the principal

school research checklist to frame some of your questions when you meet with your school's principal. Even if you were a teacher in the school or district where you are now a coach, engage in this research to help you develop a more global understanding of your school.

Meet with the Principal

Arrange a meeting with the principal(s) of the schools where you will be coaching prior to your first coaching day with teachers. If it is not possible to meet face-to-face, schedule a time to talk on the phone or communicate via email.

For teacher leaders and school-based coaches who are coaching at schools where you were teachers, even though you already have a relationship with your principal, set aside time to meet to discuss your work as coach. Once you step out of the classroom and into the role of literacy coach, your role shifts from being responsible for the education of your students to helping shape the education of other teachers' students. Opening lines of communication about coaching with your principal and establishing norms that will guide your coaching work is vital to your success.

Figure 1–3 is an example of an email I sent to a principal prior to beginning my work as a district coach. I always set goals for meetings so that the principal knows in advance what is on my mind. I bring my questions for the principal and School Research Form with me to ensure I gather the information I need.

Get Acquainted with Teachers

How you begin getting to know your teachers and their students depends so much on the culture of the school. Better to proceed with caution, feeling out how teachers regard professional development and your role as a coach, than to rush into classrooms uninvited, eager to begin your work.

Arrange to meet teachers, perhaps at a staff meeting or at a grade-level or department meeting. Be willing to share a bit about yourself and express your eagerness to be as supportive as you can. One principal introduced me to the staff during a back-to-school breakfast, which was terrific because the setting was festive and relaxed. Another principal invited me to attend a professional development session as a participant alongside teachers so that my introduction to the staff was as a fellow learner, not an "expert." A third principal asked me to be available when teachers were setting up their classrooms and offered me to teachers as a second set of hands. I got to know a number of staff members

To: Vince Riveroll (Director, Gompers Charter Middle School)
Date: August 15
Re: Upcoming work at GCMS

Hi Vince,

Thank you for finding time to have a planning conversation about my upcoming work with your Literacy teachers this school year. I am looking forward to our meeting on Monday, August 22, from 7:30–9:30.

Since I haven't worked with you or your staff before, and we have ten days scheduled between now and December, I'd like to make sure we have a chance to get clear on your goals for my work.

I did some research on GCMS on the district website, so I have some background knowledge about your students and their achievement data. With a mixture of veteran and new teachers, we'll have to be strategic about what we want teachers to know and be able to do and how we will address the needs of all of the teachers in the group. I have some ideas about how to do that and am looking forward to hearing your ideas.

I am excited that you want me to begin by leading whole-staff sessions. That way teachers can get to know me and I can get to know them. Hopefully some of the teachers will express an interest in continuing to work with me, perhaps in small-group sessions or in their classrooms.

Here's what I'd like to accomplish during our two hours together:

- Discuss your vision for teaching and learning at GCMS so I can better understand how my work fits in with your bigger picture
- Clarify what you expect your teachers and their students to know and be able to do as a result of our work
- Get a sense of what you know about what your teachers need for their learning (ex: Who learns best through demonstration? Professional reading? Side-by-side coaching? Observation?)
- Map out the goals of my first day with teachers
- Determine what the teachers think the role of a coach is

Continues

FIG. 1–3 Introductory email to a principal

I'm really looking forward to our work together. If you have any questions, please don't hesitate to ask.

By the way, I attached the NCTE article that I mentioned during our phone call, "A Call to Action: What We Know About Adolescent Literacy and Ways to Support Teachers in Meeting Students' Needs." The ideas are compelling and may influence how we design the work with your teachers.

See you soon,
Katherine

FIG. I–3 Cont.

by helping them dust off furniture, arrange classroom libraries, and staple fadeless paper to bulletin boards. A fourth had me teach a lesson with students during a whole-staff professional development session to establish some credibility and to show teachers how I might be helpful in their classrooms. Unfortunately, not all introductions go smoothly or set a collaborative tone: after one principal introduced me as, "the savior coach from the district because we're a failing school," it took all the grace I could muster to forge ahead, trying to establish trusting relationships with the teachers—and eventually succeeding. If you are coaching where you taught or teach, you have established relationships already. Still, encourage the principal to explain your coaching role to the staff so that teachers are clear on your new position.

Perhaps the culture of the school is such that teachers are accustomed to welcoming visitors into their classrooms. If so, ask the teachers with whom you'll be working when you might be able to stop by to get to know the students better.

Open lines of communication with your teachers as soon as you can. Figure 1–4 shows an email that Ryan Henderson, a school-based coach in the Highline School District in Washington, sent to his teachers after visiting their classrooms during the first weeks of school.

Staying Organized

One of the daunting challenges literacy coaches face is keeping track of everything. You will need to develop a system of organization that works for you. Here's what works for me.

To: My Colleagues
From: Ryan
Date: September 23
Re: Notes from the Coach

*I suggest that the only books that influence us are those
for which we are ready, and which have gone a little farther down
our particular path than we have yet got ourselves.*

—E.M. Forster

Hi all,

This is the end of our first two weeks. Have you noticed how stunningly beautiful these students are? I am enamored with them, and so excited to get to know them as readers and learners as I am in and out of your classrooms.

I am learning so much being in your classrooms: about your routines, about where your students are, about what your focus is as we begin the year, about how to get better and more explicit in instruction . . . It is a privilege to be accepted into your rooms and into your professional life as we learn together about reflective practice in literacy. It is exciting to discover together how we can plan, learn, and teach together. I will be participating in a coaching cycle with Sue, my coach at the district level, and will be asking to steal one of your classrooms for portions of your reading time for a week.

I am looking forward to working with Dave, Dacia, Mallory, and Anne V. next week. These will complete my round of initial visits. I have some chunks of time next Thurs. and Fri. if there are things you would like to work on or if you'd like me to observe a specific component of your literacy block. Plan for me to pop in to your room during reading block in the next week or so.

Thanks for reading. *Reply with any way that I can be of help to you.* Are you itching for me to come in and observe or experience a certain aspect of your literacy program? Are you looking for a read-aloud to meet a certain learning target? Wondering how to introduce a new genre? Do you have a specific goal and are just ready to get in and get

Continues

FIG. 1–4 Coach's communication with staff

dirty with co-planning and co-teaching? Would you like a recom-
mendation of a specific professional book that may meet your needs?
Let me know!

Gratefully,
Ryan

P.S. A huge thanks to Heather for organizing another successful
Scholastic Book Fair! I felt like I was in a prepubescent mosh pit in
there last night, and she handled the crowds with finesse.

FIG. 1–4 Cont.

A Fully Stocked Materials Container ◆ As a classroom teacher, you probably had your favorite markers and materials at your fingertips. When you
work in other people's classrooms or schools, you cannot be sure that the
materials you need will be just where you can find them. Gather your
favorites into a container that you can use whenever you teach lessons or
lead workshops. My container includes:

- ◆ A set of four chart-paper markers
- ◆ A blue and a black dry-erase marker for whiteboards
- ◆ A blue and a black washable overhead projector marker
- ◆ A pen for note taking
- ◆ A roll of blue painter's tape for hanging charts without sticking to
  anything permanently
- ◆ Magnets for hanging charts on magnetized whiteboards
- ◆ 3-by-3-inch sticky notes
- ◆ A timer to keep track of pacing

A Supply Folder ◆ Supplies are often scarce in teachers' classrooms, so try
to bring along whatever you think you will need as you teach. In a two-
pocket folder I always bring an ample supply of:

- ◆ Blank overhead transparencies to use on an overhead projector
- ◆ Blank name tags—to avoid forgetting people's names during a lesson
  or a workshop

A Folding Rolling Cart ◆ You probably need some kind of rolling cart or
bag to carry around your supplies and binders. I use a folding rolling cart that
looks like a milk crate on wheels.

A Digital Camera ◆ Bring a digital camera wherever you go and you will have a much easier time keeping a record of your work. While you may want to save a co-constructed chart you make with a group of students or teachers to show other educators, the learning recorded on the chart should be left with the learners. Or you may come across student work that you want to save but cannot because it belongs to the student and you run out of time to photocopy it. A digital camera enables you to take a quick photo of your

FIG. 1–5 A rolling cart to carry supplies

charts, student work, classroom environments, or students or adults at work. Ask permission, of course, before taking any photos. Store the images on your computer or print them out and include photos in your binders.

I use digital photos to help me remember what I worked on with people and to help communicate with others about my work. Two years ago I worked as a district coach with over a dozen middle schools, often coaching in classrooms with middle school teachers from a variety of schools observing, and occasionally leading professional development sessions for the teachers and their principals. Whenever possible, principals observed my coaching work and attended my sessions. Because of scheduling issues, the same group of middle school teachers could not always be present, though the work we were doing together was cumulative and everyone wanted to stay on track. Keeping everybody informed about the classroom coaching work and professional development sessions seemed daunting until I started photographing charts and samples of student work. By uploading the photos to a photosharing website and emailing everyone a brief summary of the day's work and a link to the photosharing website, people stayed informed. Plus, teachers and principals started uploading their own photos to show how they were applying the ideas from our work together in their own classrooms and schools, adding to what we could all learn.

Binders and Notebooks ◆ The number of binders and notebooks you need depends on how detailed you plan to be with record keeping. At the least, school-based coaches and teacher leaders need a binder for each teacher; district coaches, a binder for each school with sections for each teachers; and consultants, a binder for each district with sections for each school or group of teachers.

I use a two-inch binder labeled with the school's name. I take notes on three-hole-punched notepads that are stored in the binders. Each binder has sections for:

- ◆ School information
  - School research form
  - Teacher schedules, classroom locations
  - School map
  - Any pertinent policies or procedures
  - Schedule of school events such as half-days or assemblies
  - Testing dates
- ◆ Communication with the principal
  - Copies of emails
  - Notes from meetings

- ◆ Each teacher
  - Copies of communication with the teacher
  - Student data sheet
  - Student observation forms
  - Prebrief planning sheets
  - Post-lesson planning sheets
  - Next-steps planning sheets
  - Observation notes
  - Lesson plans

You may also need binders to store the materials you need to conduct professional development sessions. For example, on one of my professional development shelves I have binders labeled writing workshop, learning to read, reading assessment, guided reading, writing assessment, interpretation, and critical literacy.

In each professional development binder I also store materials related to the topic such as:

- ◆ Articles from professional journals
- ◆ Recommended texts
- ◆ Overheads, agendas, and handouts I created to use in professional development sessions
- ◆ Samples or photos of student work or co-constructed charts

Know that as your work evolves, so, too, will your systems of organization. Err on the side of saving as much as you can, since the materials will come in handy as your work continues and can serve as a record of your work to date.

 ## You *Are* a Coach

Becoming comfortable as a literacy coach will come, just as becoming comfortable as a teacher came, with experience and effort. You can build your confidence and your potential for effectiveness by developing systems of organization, establishing relationships with members of the school community, and researching the school and district. By maintaining a collaborative and reflective stance, opening lines of communication, and better understanding what coaches need to know and be able to do, you are on your way to success.

What a Coach Needs to Know and Be Able to Do

The role of literacy coach is a complex one that shifts and changes in response to the culture of your school, your teachers' needs, and your continually evolving knowledge and skills. Use what follows, based on the International Reading Association's (2006) professional standards for literacy coaches, on research about effective coaching, and on my own experience with literacy coaching, to better understand what you need to know and be able to do.

 ## Literacy Coaches Strive to Improve Student Achievement by Supporting Teaching and Learning

The literacy coach's role is the same as every adult's role in the education system: to provide all children with the highest-quality education possible. Every decision a coach makes and every action a coach takes aims at improving the quality of teaching in order to improve the quality of student learning.

Here is my theory of action. While some students are learning at high levels, we know that large groups of children are not learning in our schools today, giving rise to much conversation about our persistent achievement gap. The national conversation about the state of American education is rife with research documenting the failure of schools to provide all students with highly qualified teachers who teach effectively. The increasing federalization of public education under the No Child Left Behind Act is one of many responses to a growing concern about the continuing failure of our schools.

Just look in the classrooms at your school and ask yourself, "Are all students learning at the highest level they can?" Without a doubt, your answer is no. We know that many factors contribute to the crisis, including poverty, lack of access to high-quality early childhood literacy experiences, and high mobility rates (Viadero 2000). Many factors are out of our control. We cannot change the experiences students have had or not had before they arrive in our classrooms. What we can control is the quality of teaching that we provide when our students are in our classrooms.

We know that it is teachers' expertise—their knowledge and skill—that produces student learning. Linda Darling-Hammond writes, "research indicates that the effects of well-prepared teachers on student achievement can be stronger than the influences of student background factors, such as poverty, language background, and minority status" (1999, 39). If the level of student learning is not acceptable, then we need to improve the quality of our teaching. We need to boost our expertise, change practice, and add increasingly effective strategies and skills that will produce profound improvement in student learning.

As soon as the word *improvement* enters the teaching conversation, we tend to get defensive, because to suggest we need to improve implies that what we are doing right now is not good enough. Yet we know that what we are currently doing isn't meeting every child's needs, and even though we proclaim that we believe "all children can learn," we know that we are failing large groups of students. While acknowledging that our students' literacy skills are lacking, we feel unprepared to teach literacy, especially if we presumed our upper elementary, middle, and high school students would come to us already reading and writing well. A group of middle school teachers with whom I work emailed me a refrain I've heard time and time again: "We didn't sign up to be teachers of reading! Or to teach writing! We know how to be teachers of social studies, science, and English and now everything is changing. Our students are struggling and we want to help them but *how*? *when*? Will you *help* us?" What we are doing in classrooms may be the best we know how to do, given the knowledge and skills we have right now. But our current best simply is not enough for many students.

The need for improvement shouldn't be seen as an attack or criticism but as a ray of hope as teachers strive to educate all students. If we believe it is our teaching, and not "teacher-proofed" curriculum materials or programs, that produces student learning, then improving our teaching to improve student learning is part of the act of teaching itself. The process must to be embedded in our practice so that we reflect after each lesson on evidence of student learning to decide what students need next.

What is insulting and defeating is telling an educator to improve her practice without providing the necessary support to do so. Throughout my teaching years I attended professional development sessions that left me near tears, frustrated because the facilitator made me aware of all I wasn't yet doing for my students without teaching me the knowledge and skills I needed to remedy the situation. Resounding in my head were statements like *show me how to improve . . . come work with me in my classroom . . . help me find the materials I need*. I didn't want or need people just to *tell* me how to improve my teaching. I begged people to *show* me, to work alongside me with my students, to help me problem-solve, and to guide me through the inevitable roller coaster of feelings associated with the process of change.

Our role as literacy coaches is to work side-by-side with teachers, in their classrooms with their students, to provide them with the support they need to improve their instruction and increase their students' knowledge and skill. Our role is to *show* teachers, not simply talk about, effective teaching strategies. Our role is to analyze teachers' students as learners, determine their strengths and needs, analyze teachers as learners, make decisions about what both need next for their learning, carefully plan how to structure the learning, and then teach both students and teacher. In short, our role is to apply what we know about best teaching practices to our coaching work.

Literacy Coaches Learn and Teach Effective Decision Making

Effective teaching requires making countless decisions that change from student to student, day to day, and minute to minute. The art of teaching is the art of making decisions with the child at the center in the teaching-learning cycle. Teaching involves determining what students already know and are able to do so that lessons always build on a foundation of student strengths. Teaching involves determining what students need next for their learning, and then deciding what would be the most effective and efficient way to teach a lesson to meet these needs. Teaching also involves determining what the evidence of understanding will look and sound like, then assessing that understanding and making adjustments. After each lesson, teachers reflect on their teaching and what students have learned, examining evidence to determine what needs to happen in the next lesson, and the cycle begins again.

Similarly, effective coaching requires countless decisions that change from teacher to teacher, day to day, and minute to minute. The art of coaching is the art of making decisions with the students *and teachers* at the center of every decision. Coaching involves determining what students and teachers already know and are able to do so that coaching opportunities always build on a foundation of teacher and student strengths. It involves determining what students and teachers need next for their learning, making decisions about what would be the most effective and efficient way to coach, determining what evidence of understanding looks and sounds like so that the coach can be responsive to what the students and teachers need. Coaching involves reflection on the teaching and learning, examining evidence that demonstrates student and teacher learning, to determine what needs to happen next in the coaching work.

Textbooks and curricula do not teach students—teachers do. Regardless of the curriculum materials teachers use for their teaching, it is the moment-by-moment decisions teachers make as they teach that result in student learning. The role of the literacy coach is to support teachers as they become increasingly effective decision makers and, since teachers have a variety of needs and learning styles, literacy coaches should be prepared to provide support in a variety of forms.

 ## Literacy Coaches Learn and Teach Literacy Content Knowledge

Developing your own literacy content knowledge so that you can help develop your teachers' literacy content knowledge is one of your primary coaching roles. Just because you have been a successful classroom teacher and have now been made a coach doesn't necessarily mean that you already know enough about literacy development to lead others. Plus, what you already know may not be sufficient going forward. The definition of literacy isn't static. Broadly defined as "the ability to read and write" (www.dictionary.com), our understanding of literacy is dynamic and evolving to include critical literacy, media literacy, visual literacy, and informational literacy, to name a few. Be open to learning, since you'll need to continually gain knowledge and skill.

Occasionally I hear educators attribute my knowledge about literacy to "being a born literacy teacher," or "being really smart" and, while that seems flattering on the surface, the comments actually belie the amount of work, study, and determination required of any of us to continually hone our teaching practice. I started my preservice teacher education program certain that I never wanted to be responsible for teaching children to read. Too much pressure, too much room to mess up a child's life in my first few years of teaching, I reasoned. What I learned in my reading methods classes espoused research that stated, "Students learn to read in grades K–3 and then read to learn in fourth grade and beyond." Relieved I could avoid teaching reading, I based my decision to teach fourth or fifth grade on the belief that by then students would already know how to read. Blissfully unaware of the importance of the coursework that focused on teaching primary reading, I did enough to get an A in my courses, but not enough to concentrate on the complexity of teaching children to read. And then I became a woefully unprepared classroom teacher of third and fourth graders, of whom the majority were reading at a first-grade level. Undeterred, and still believing the learn-to-read, read-to-learn mantra, I decided to try moving up to fifth grade the next year so that I could teach "readers." I simply didn't know that learning to read is a lifelong process. Certainly not the hallmark of a born literacy teacher.

With the support of staff developers who worked alongside me in my classroom, by attending professional development sessions, by reading professional texts, and by becoming an acute observer of students as they learned, I began to learn how to teach students to be literate. The research debunked, I now know that learning to read is always about reading to learn. Even if I had paid close attention in my reading methods class, I would have had to engage in rigorous professional study because the reality we face in the classroom is always more complex than anything we learn in the abstract. I am still learning to teach students to read and write and to increase my content knowledge. Yours will increase, too, as you engage in professional study.

 ## Literacy Coaches Learn and Teach Pedagogical Content Knowledge

As teachers make decisions, one guiding question is *what do my students need to know and be able to do?* Answering this question helps teachers determine the content (the what). A second question, *how will I get them there?* focuses on the pedagogical process (the how). Increasing pedagogical skills is essential as coaches increase content knowledge because one is useless without the other. Coaches can have a tremendous amount of content knowledge about literacy, but without pedagogical skills—for teaching both students *and* adults—

teaching and learning in the classroom will not be effective. Conversely, exemplary teaching skills devoid of the right content are not useful, either.

"Coaches themselves need to be excellent teachers in the same discipline as the teacher being coached, able to provide situation-specific assistance adapted to that teacher" (West and Staub 2003, 1). The teachers you coach will want to see you teach their students successfully, and being able to do so is one of the quickest ways to establish trust. Lyons and Pinnell (2001) identify trust as one of the critical factors in a coaching relationship, and trust is a nuanced and complex issue within coaching that will be addressed throughout this book. Some teachers may be wary of your credentials and your ability to offer them anything useful to use with their students. You may hear people say, "Oh, this wouldn't work with *my* students," or "What does this coach have to offer me?" When you actually get into teachers' classrooms, demonstrate pedagogical moves that meet the needs of their students, handle classroom management issues that arise, and teach students to know and be able to do something the classroom teacher believes is useful and necessary, you begin to establish trust.

How do you build your knowledge of and performance in pedagogy? Read professional texts that describe pedagogy and then try the ideas with students. Analyze exemplary lessons, tease out what the teacher and students are doing that yields such success, and try on the ideas with students. Study learning theory, how students learn to read and write, and infuse that knowledge into lessons you design. Be reflective about your own lessons, name what supported students and what got in the way, brainstorm ways to improve your lessons, and then try on the improvements. Develop an understanding of the questioning strategies, tasks, and classroom structures that help students grow and develop ideas and skills.

If you are new to coaching and relatively new to the teaching profession, your confidence may be shaky. Even if you are an experienced teacher, the reality of being expected to teach lessons to unfamiliar students across a wide range of grade levels or departments may make you nervous. Find a class of students to be your practice group and carve out time to spend improving your pedagogy. How do you find such a class? Ask a colleague who supports your work and with whom you feel comfortable if you can visit periodically to try on lessons. Explain to your colleague that you want to improve your skills, try out ideas before sharing them with teachers, and experiment with ideas you read in professional texts. Brand-new teachers are often eager to watch an experienced teacher work with their students. Establish relationships with teachers and students so that you have a regular place to hone your craft.

Literacy Coaches Learn How to Be Effective Teachers of Adults

Not only do you need to be an effective teacher of students, you also need to be an effective teacher of adults. If you just left the classroom to become a literacy coach, you may have limited experience teaching adults. A steep part of your learning curve will include developing your teaching repertoire for teaching adults. Luckily, much of what you already know about effective teaching applies to adults. Hold on to what you know about good instruction as you begin your coaching work. If we believe all children can learn, then we must believe that everyone at any age has the potential to learn. Like children, adults thrive when they are motivated and actively engaged in learning opportunities that meet their needs, which is why so much of our coaching work focuses on determining what teachers need next for their learning and how to design effective learning opportunities.

Adult learners do differ in some ways from young learners (Knowles, Holton, and Swanson 2005), and you may stumble across these differences immediately in your coaching work. Lyons and Pinnell explain, "Adults have acquired ideas, beliefs, values, and passions about learning, developed after years of success and perhaps failure during the years they have spent in schools" (2001, 3). I continually remind myself that what teachers know and believe about teaching and learning have been shaped not only by their teaching years but also by their years as students of many teachers. Why should I think that a professional development session or two (or many, for that matter) is going to suddenly shift a teacher's beliefs? At the same time, adults are goal oriented and want to problem-solve solutions to issues facing them, so I keep in mind that when I can craft adult learning opportunities that capitalize on teachers' motivation to problem-solve, our professional study can shift knowledge, skill, and beliefs. Chapter 7 focuses closely on guiding principles for designing adult learning.

Literacy Coaches Strive to Build Teaching and Leadership Capacity

For all children to have access to high-quality teaching and learning, it is not enough for the literacy coach and a few teachers to hold the knowledge and skill about effective literacy instruction. Plus, as Linda Lambert (1998, 3) explains, "as long as improvement is dependent on a single person or a few people or outside direction and forces, it will fail." Providing professional development opportunities designed to reach a significant number of teachers is one way to begin to build teachers' capacity to meet all students' needs.

Another way is for the literacy coach to determine which teachers have instructional strengths in particular areas and the willingness to work with the coach and colleagues to help build capacity. With support from the coach, the teacher can begin to take the lead on working with colleagues to share her knowledge and skill.

A kindergarten teacher approached me because she wanted to know more about using interactive writing to support English Language Learners. I demonstrated interactive writing and coached her as she tried the approach with her students. Within two weeks the teacher confidently incorporated interactive writing into her daily literacy block and piqued the curiosity of her colleagues with her enthusiastic reports of student successes.

I approached the kindergarten teacher to ask her if she would be willing to help me build the capacity of the kindergarten team by first introducing them to interactive writing and then by demonstrating lessons for her colleagues and helping them plan their own instruction. Together we planned a series of grade-level meetings, gradually decreasing my role as a coach and increasing her role as the kindergarten interactive writing teacher leader. Building the capacity of one teacher helped build the capacity of an entire grade-level team.

Literacy Coaches Embrace Resistance

Like our students, adults are actively or passively vocal about what they need for their learning. Our role is to really hear their concerns and use the information to improve our work with teachers. We can be so quick to deem people resistant to change. Teachers raise concerns or don't immediately implement the ideas we generate during professional development, and we conclude they don't want to change. But are they resistant or just thoughtful, inquisitive educators who need more information, research, examples, experiences, or support, who are reflecting the limitations of our professional development sessions, and who are trying to make meaning of the implications for their work with their students?

During our teacher-leader training sessions, whenever we complained about teachers who were, in our opinions, resistant to change, my coach Lucy

West implored, "Don't silence resistance. Embrace resistance. Listen to resistance. Within what you are calling resistance lies what you need to do." Huh? Embrace resistance? Part of the reason I shied away from asking teachers if they had any questions or concerns about our work was because I didn't want to open a Pandora's box and now Lucy wanted me to embrace resistance? (I admit it, I even avoided using exit slips to get teachers' feedback after sessions because I was afraid of what they might say about our work in general and my coaching work in particular.) It took me a while to learn that I learn more from people who disagree with me.

Lucy taught me that I don't have to have an answer for every question, a solution for every problem right then, in the moment. Instead, I need to jot down what teachers say (or don't say), reflect on the comments, and use the comments to inform my decision making about upcoming work and to evaluate the effectiveness of my past coaching work (Figure 2–1). Here's an example. A group of eighth-grade teachers gathered to continue to co-plan nonfiction reading lessons. Two weeks earlier, our examination of the reading standards revealed a heavy emphasis on students' being able to find the similarities and differences between the scope, sequence, and treatment of ideas in texts and on teaching students to evaluate the credibility, logic, and validity of an author's argument. Teachers concluded that though they expect students to use nonfiction texts when writing research reports, they don't currently teach students how to be critical readers of nonfiction texts. Teachers requested planning time and agreed to bring nonfiction materials they thought would be useful in their students' nonfiction study. During our first session, we planned a few lessons, and within a few days, I taught one in each of the four teachers' classrooms. As we worked together during our second planning session, I noted their comments and questions, and tried not to get too frustrated when it seemed that the lessons I taught weren't effective.

When I reviewed my teachers' comments, I realized why the teachers were hesitant to change their instructional practice: they needed more support. I was frustrated that my work with scheduling time and my demonstration lessons weren't enough and, rather than conclude that my coaching just wasn't explicit enough to be effective, was tempted to blame my teachers for not understanding the work or being resistant to change. But after I calmed down, I shifted from reacting to their comments to creating an action plan to better meet their needs.

Embracing resistance turned out to be great coaching advice. It taught me that what I think is resistance is not resistance at all, but often just an indicator of what teachers need next for their learning. I encourage you to take

Teacher's comments	My thoughts	Action plan
"Not enough materials for students to do this well. Where are we going to instead get more texts students can read?"	I agree. Finding multiple texts that address the same topic is difficult. We need to teach students to find texts that interest them.	Request that the school librarian revisit how to find materials. Or, instead of demonstrating one of the lessons, maybe I can do the finding materials lesson with students in the library.
"When are we ever going to find the time to do this work in the classroom?"	I guess the work we did on scheduling time for instruction last session wasn't enough.	Revisit scheduling. Ask teachers who have figured out scheduling to share with colleagues.
"This isn't going to work for my students. They need much more scaffolding."	What does the teacher mean by more scaffolding?	Find time to have a conversation with teacher.
"What if kids aren't interested in the topics we use for our modeling?"	What if?	Not sure.
"I'm really worried that we're devoting a lot of time to this study and it is never going to work. I'll try it, but I'm telling you, I'm worried this isn't going to work. Why? Because I just can't picture it happening and you know how I am when I can't see the big picture."	Did a demonstration lesson in her room last week. Talked about the big picture of the non-fiction study. Must not have been clear enough.	Need to schedule time to talk big picture again.
"These materials have lots of unfamiliar vocab. What about our English Language Learners? I'm thinking they'll be totally lost."	Included ELL supports in my demo—maybe teacher has a different idea about supports? Didn't notice my supports?	Videotape demo in teacher's classroom so we can talk about the ELL supports (and to show the team, since they teach ELLs, too).

FIG. 2–1 Reflective notes on teachers' comments

Lucy's advice, since listening for your teachers' concerns will help shape and improve your coaching work, too. As Andrew Gitlin and Frank Margonis state, "We believe teachers' initial expressions of cynicism about reform should not automatically be viewed as obstructionist acts to overcome. Instead, time should be spent looking carefully at those resistant acts to see if they might embody a form of good sense—potential insights into the root causes of why the more things change the more they stay the same" (1995, 224).

Literacy Coaches Are Effective Communicators

Effective communication is crucial: leading professional development sessions, conducting pre- and post-conferences, meeting with the principal, giving teachers feedback, engaging in conversation with teachers and students and their families, sharing our beliefs, arranging visitations—the list of times we need to communicate with others seems endless. Our communication ranges from discussing logistics and schedules and materials to our beliefs about teaching and learning. Since much of coaching work involves writing notes or emails, not just live, face-to-face communication, we need to be effective communicators in person as well as in writing. In Chapter 1 and in the following chapters I've included a variety of transcripts of conversations and examples of written communication to give you samples of coaches' communication styles to consider as you continue to develop your own voice as a literacy coach.

One of your roles is to talk in front of large and small groups of adults. Videotape and watch sessions you lead to see if you are clear, engaging, well paced, and responsive. Yes, you'll cringe watching yourself on tape, but seeing your strengths and identifying your needs will pay off as you work to improve your presentation skills. Better to cringe at your image on screen than to cringe hearing people quote you saying what you didn't mean to say. Rest assured you will grow more comfortable speaking to large or small groups of adults by doing it more often.

Because I have experienced how language can clarify or cloud understanding, I actively work at becoming a more effective communicator and consider myself a "collector of language." As I listen to people speak or read their emails, I pay attention to what they say, how their message affects me, and how they put together language. And when statements make me say, "Hmm . . . that was well said," I scribble down words. For example, when my colleague Lyn Reggett explained that as we plan instruction, "we have to figure out what students need for their learning, which is different from what students need to learn,"

I thought about the wisdom in that statement for weeks. Subtle, yet profound. I also notice when others around me react negatively to statements or misunderstand ideas, then I try to figure out why and write down what not to say. As you coach, heighten your awareness of what you and others are saying, listen for understanding as well as misunderstanding, and analyze how your language affects others. Effective communication matters.

Literacy Coaches Communicate Their Beliefs and Provide a Rationale

Your role requires you to provide and communicate a rationale about why the improvement of instruction is essential. Teachers will repeatedly question why they need to change their practice, why what they have always done is not "good enough anymore," and they should, since understanding the rationale is vital. As you coach, your beliefs will be constantly challenged, and in your most frustrating moments, in the moments when everyone and everything seem to conspire against you in your role, your beliefs about teaching and learning will steady you. What do you believe about literacy, how students learn, the curriculum materials your teachers may be using, and the feasibility of teaching all students to be literate? What do you really believe about the coaching work you've agreed to do?

Here's what I know and return to when questions come at me rapid-fire. "What's wrong with the way we were taught? If the education I received was good enough for me, why are you saying it isn't good enough for my students?" Good questions. Here's what I don't say: "We're doing this because the district says so, or because the principal says so, or because NCLB says so, or because the curriculum materials say so." There's nothing inspiring or grounded in the "so-and-so says so" justification. As I think about the questions, a couple of responses come to mind. First, we are preparing students for their future, not our past. And our students' future, actually their present, is starkly different from what we experienced at their age. Bombarded by instant access to an abundance of information through the Internet and other media outlets, students must be skilled, critical readers and listeners of informational texts and highly effective oral and written communicators in a variety of forms including emails, text messages, instant messaging, and blogs. The literacy instruction I received that focused on heavy doses of reading and writing fiction, with scant attention paid to reading and writing informational texts beyond writing research reports about teacher-assigned topics, barely prepared me for the rigors of college and certainly isn't sufficient for students in this day and age. Second, for whom was education successful? Your teachers' methods may have reached you and other students, too, but which students fell through the cracks? I moved from second through eighth grade with the same eighty students. I can still list the names of the students who barely made it through elementary and middle school. We need to improve our teaching because the answer to the question, "For whom is education successful?" should always have been, and now really needs to be, "all students." Not because of NCLB, but because every student has a right to a high-quality education, and we can control how we educate students when they are in our school.

Jot down the hard questions teachers ask and, when you have moments to reflect, think about your beliefs, what you know to be true, and practice crafting responses that communicate your rationale for why you are doing whatever you are doing.

Literacy Coaches Are Evaluators of Literacy Needs

In order to design effective instruction, teachers need to use ongoing assessments to gauge their students' strengths and areas of need. As a classroom teacher you learned that figuring out what students know and are able to do is a multifaceted process involving the use of a variety of assessment methods. Now you are instrumental in helping teachers use a range of assessment tools to make informed decisions about students' literacy needs. You may be administering and using assessment tools that are unfamiliar, which is why I suggest you download or locate as much information as you can about the formal assessments your teachers use. Coaching also involves helping teachers assess students in the moment, by conferring; using running records; observing students at work; listening to student talk; analyzing written work; using benchmark tests, student surveys, reading inventories; and so on. I needed my colleagues' and literacy coach's help figuring out how to analyze and use the assessment information I gathered and stacked in precariously high piles in the back of my classroom. You need to bring teachers together to problem-solve how to use assessment data to monitor student progress and inform instructional planning.

In addition to evaluating the literacy needs of students within specific classrooms, coaches need to look at the broad strokes that data can reveal about teaching and learning by grade level, department, and whole school. Are there particular genres students write well and others less well or not at all? Does reading instruction focus on some skills and strategies to the exclusion of others? Are students progressing in their listening and speaking skills? Are English Language Learners acquiring written and oral language proficiency at an acceptable rate? These are among the questions I keep in mind when I try to identify patterns and trends. Chapter 4 looks more closely at analyzing data to inform professional development decisions. Keep in mind that evaluating literacy needs occurs not just when you gather with other educators at your school to look at formal and informal assessment data, but also every time you analyze instruction and ask, "What do students know and what are they able to do as a result of this lesson?"

Literacy Coaches Inspire and Lead

In the quiet moments of our day, when we can put aside the nagging list of things to do, issues to tackle, teachers to support, insecurities to soothe, challenges to face, let's remember that literacy coaching is about the students who look to us, to their teachers, and to their school community for an education. Let's keep our eye on the prize—educating *all* students. Certainly the challenges our teachers face are daunting, which is all the more reason for us to join them, by their side, to contribute significant support to their efforts. Let's inspire and lead instructional improvement. Michael Fullan writes, "whatever the case, effective leaders make people feel that even the most difficult problems can be tackled productively. They are always hopeful—conveying a sense of optimism and an attitude of never giving up in the pursuit of highly valued goals. Their enthusiasm and confidence (not certainty) are, in a word, infectious, and they are infectiously effective . . ." (2001, 7). Let's figure out how to be infectiously effective.

Building a Relationship with Your Principal

Before we address strategies for coaching teachers, let's consider the leadership situation in any school you might enter. You may encounter a principal with strong literacy knowledge and skill. Or perhaps the principal has a desire to learn about literacy and will be learning alongside teachers as you coach and lead professional development sessions. Thrilled to finally have a coach, your principal may have greeted you with a coaching plan shaped by teachers. Perhaps you work with a principal who is delighted to have a coach but unsure of how to use a coach effectively, and you anticipate having to figure out your coaching work together. Or perhaps you work with a principal who resists having a coach or having to focus on literacy at all. If your district assigns coaches to schools labeled "failing" or, even worse, to principals labeled "failing," your principal may resent your presence, see you as a spy for the district, and actively or passively undermine your work. Ouch. This chapter addresses such harsh realities, along with happier, more typical situations.

The following ideas about building a relationship with your principal apply to your coaching supervisor, too, if you have one. However you became a coach, and whether or not you also report to a coaching supervisor, the relationship that you build with the principal of each school in which you work is essential to the ultimate goal of increasing the quality of education for all students.

 ## Why a Whole Chapter on Building Your Relationship with Your Principal?

Literacy coaching is about improving literacy learning for all students, and principal leadership really matters in school improvement. Michael Fullan writes, "I know of no improving school that doesn't have a principal who is good at leading improvement. 'Almost every single study of school effectiveness has shown both primary and secondary leadership to be a key factor,' says Sammons (1999) in her major review" (2000, 141). Whether or not your principal is open to learning with and from you, your responsibility is to approach your work as if your principal will, over time, be influenced by your work. If we believe all students can learn, let's perform our work with the belief that all teachers and all principals can learn, too.

Be prepared to teach your principal about literacy. Though principals are not expected to know as much about literacy teaching and learning as you and your teachers are, they do need to know enough to be able to make informed decisions about how to lead and support literacy work, from how to release funds for substitute teachers so your teachers can attend professional development, to why they need to purchase literacy materials, to why it may be noisier in classrooms as students construct meaning of texts, to how to make fair and reasonable assessments of instructional practice during classroom evaluations. Building a relationship with your principal also helps you understand, and perhaps influence, the school culture in which your teachers work.

Some coaches may be tempted to skip this chapter, since some districts explicitly or implicitly deemphasize coaches' relationships with principals out of concern that teachers will associate coaching with evaluation. I acknowledge and have experienced what happens when the line blurs between coaching and evaluation, when principals misuse coaches, or when coaches do not respect the boundary between coaching and supervision—when educators and students get hurt by the missteps of others—but I do not believe the solution is to keep teachers, literacy coaches, and principals apart. Instead, I believe the solution is to work to establish healthy relationships with clear boundaries and communication so that all adults are working together toward instructional improvement.

Establish and Maintain Clear Boundaries

Let's start with boundaries as the first step toward building a relationship with your principal. Neither administrator nor classroom teacher, literacy coaches exist in a kind of no man's land, traversing the bumpy terrain that results from uncertainty about roles and boundaries. You have to help establish and maintain boundaries that can become easily blurred. Teachers may see you as a conduit of information to the principal: "Can't you talk to the principal about how we're feeling?" "Would you *please* clarify what the principal meant by what he said?" "I'm having such a hard time with the principal and really want your help." Principals may treat you like a conduit, too: "Let the teachers know I expect to see changes. Find out from the grade level why students aren't making progress." You may work with principals who are indiscreet, gossip about or slam teachers, or try to undermine their work. And teachers may do the same with each other and the principal. As tempting as it may be to say, "Ohh . . . gossip . . . tell me" or to sigh, "You know, I agree with you, so and so *is* being ridiculous" or to be the conduit to win the favor of others, don't compromise the trust you are trying to build. If you gossip about the principal with the teachers, won't the teachers wonder if you gossip with the principal about them?

Draw very clear boundaries. When teachers and principals treat me like a pipeline, I respond with a variation of the same message: "If you have an issue with the principal, talk to the principal. If you have an issue with a teacher, talk to the teacher. If you have an issue with me, I'm ready to listen." Fiercely enforce these clear boundaries, even—and especially—when it feels awkward and really hard to do.

When anyone, principals and teachers alike, starts gossiping, divulging personal or personnel information, venting about people directly to or around me, I interrupt and say, "What you're talking about is making me uncomfortable. I can't be a part of (or overhear) this conversation." Sometimes people look at me funny and stop, other times people laugh and continue, and then I have to repeat myself or leave. No matter how awkward I feel in the moment, though, I never feel as strange as when I see the person who was the topic of the conversation I shouldn't have heard.

Effective literacy coaching depends on building trusting relationships with all the members of your school community. Establishing and maintaining clear boundaries goes a long way in doing that.

 ## Understand the Principal's Vision for the School

Because the principal is the person who is ultimately accountable for the student achievement and teacher practice at the school, you cannot be completely effective without a strong working relationship with her or him. Like any relationship, it takes work, open lines of communication, compromise, and collaboration.

Just as when you teach in a classroom, you want to know as much about the students as possible, when you coach, you must know as much about the school from the principal's point of view as possible. Even if you were a teacher in the school where you are now a coach and you think you know a great deal about your school, you will be amazed at how much you do not know until you get the bird's-eye view from the principal's perspective.

As you begin your coaching work, have conversations with the principal. Here are some questions I suggest you ask, my rationale for asking them, and some sample answers. Some of the questions may strike you as more personal or sensitive than others, so use your judgment about which ones make sense to ask and when.

What Are Your Beliefs About Learning and Teaching?

The principal's beliefs set the tone for the work at a school. Every educator has beliefs about teaching and learning, and you need to figure out the degree to which your beliefs match your principal's vision of teaching and learning. You may hear statements such as:

◆ Students learn best through a process approach to the teaching of reading and writing.

◆ Teachers need to be strong decision makers so that they can be responsive to students' needs as they teach.

◆ Students will learn best when teachers follow our new textbook adoption.

◆ English Learners need additional supports, which are best delivered by grouping similarly skilled students together.

◆ English Learners need to be immersed in classrooms with high levels of academic language so that they have models to emulate.

◆ It doesn't matter what I believe because the district just tells us what to do.

◆ Students need to be actively engaged in cognitively demanding tasks in order to learn.

◆ Because our students are underperforming, students need to make more than a year's growth in a year's time so that they won't fall further behind.

◆ All students can learn—we are working hard to address our diverse learners' needs.

◆ Teachers need time to collaborate so that they can learn from each other's strengths and successes.

◆ We are never done learning, which is why teachers are engaged in ongoing professional development.

When your beliefs differ from the principal's, try not to judge or position yourself in opposition; instead, begin to determine where you have common ground and note the principal's belief statements for future use. Think about how the beliefs are shaping the school culture to get a sense of what teachers may be experiencing.

I recently worked with a principal who said repeatedly during our initial conversation, "I want my classrooms to be quiet places where students are listening to their teachers and doing their work at their desks." In contrast, I believe that in order to learn to construct meaning as readers and to communicate meaning as writers, students need ample opportunities to think and talk together about what they are reading and writing and that to facilitate talk, students should be gathered together in a common meeting space. Instead of panicking because we appeared to have conflicting beliefs, I considered the beliefs underpinning that statement and decided that the principal wants teachers teaching and students listening, working, and learning—and so do I.

The following week, the principal observed me demonstrating a lesson on how to help students learn strategies for reading a textbook, and I asked her to note when I was expecting students to listen to me and to their classmates, and to consider the role of talking as students did their work. Later that day, when I met with the principal to discuss the lesson I taught I began by saying, "In our initial meeting, I remember how you emphasized that you want classrooms to be quiet places where students are listening to their teachers and doing their work. My lesson today was not quiet because of all the children talking. What are you thinking about my lesson and the amount of talk?" The principal was excited that all students contributed to the lesson and shared that she places a premium on quiet classrooms because in the past, classrooms were noisy because they were chaotic. To help support the principal's vision for her school, I noted to myself to continue to demonstrate in lessons how to value student voices and conversation without letting student talk get out of hand.

Through discussion of the lessons I demonstrated and our beliefs about learning and teaching, we realized that our visions are more similar than different. My lesson broadened the principal's vision of learning and teaching, and our conversation broadened my understanding of the school's history and the context in which I coached.

My early work with a principal who resented having a coach also involved demonstrating lessons. During our first conversation, the principal's responses to most of my questions sounded like, "What do my beliefs matter? The district is telling me what to do. Clearly we don't have strengths, since we're considered failing. And I don't trust the direction the district is taking us in. I just want you to do what you're supposed to do as a coach." Yikes! Though I just wanted to flee the conversation and the school, I tried to keep in mind that the principal did not necessarily dislike me (we had just met); instead, the principal disliked what I symbolized. How could I help the principal see me not as a district spy, but as a teacher, as someone who wants to work with students and teachers? How could I get the focus off animosity and distrust and onto students? How could we start to build a civil, if not yet collaborative, working relationship out of the view of the staff in case our first attempts at finding common ground were rocky?

I decided that asking the principal to observe and give me feedback on lessons might be a way to start to build common ground. Observing a lesson would enable the principal to get a sense of how I teach and see me working with children and talking with the students' teacher. Getting the principal's feedback would help me gauge the principal's knowledge of instruction and literacy, what the principal values, and how the principal communicates. Mustering up my courage, I explained to the principal that to get to know students and teachers, I would like to have a chance to teach a few lessons in a willing teacher's classroom. I further explained that I wanted the principal to get to know me as a teacher and asked the principal to come observe my teaching. After an agonizingly long pause, the principal shared that a brand-new teacher recently requested support, suggested that I approach the teacher myself, and two days later, the principal observed me teaching an interactive read-aloud lesson with second graders. Though the principal did not really observe me teach (checked email, took a phone call, and chatted with the teacher for most of the lesson), the whole experience, especially the feedback conversation, pushed the communication door ajar. I share this experience not so you think I've got patience and professionalism in spades (I don't, my instinct then and for a long time after was to avoid dealing with the principal at all), but to illustrate how I tried to begin to handle a potentially hostile and personally challenging situation. You'll have challenges to face, too. As a literacy coach, you can't avoid working with the principal if you want your work to take hold across the school. And the only way you can forge a stronger relationship with a principal is to be communicative, strategic, and persistent.

What Is Currently Going Well with Learning and Teaching?

When discussing anyone—students, teachers, families—we should start with what people *can* do and what is going well rather than what people cannot do and what is not going well. We can build on strengths. In your meetings with the principal, frame your conversation around strengths before moving toward areas of need.

Asking what is going well will give you insight into what makes the principal proud and what teachers, grade levels, and students are doing well. You can get a sense of how the school works—what teachers and families value, which teachers collaborate and how, where grade levels or departments are concentrating their efforts, which subjects may be areas of focus, which adult learning structures are working, which students are achieving, and so on. Try to get a sense of what teachers are studying, why, and in which adult learning structures. You will want to capitalize on structures that are already resulting in change in classroom practice. Begin to identify teacher leaders so that you can determine who can help you build capacity.

Here's a list of strengths written by a group of principals in one of my districts:

◆ Kindergarten teachers have taken on interactive writing! You should see what kindergartners are writing, and it is only January.

◆ Our focus on planning lessons with specific supports for English Learners is paying off. Students are acquiring language more rapidly than last year and teachers feel more focused and purposeful in how they scaffold language development.

◆ We've had four Parent Literacy meetings on the same topic—one before school, one during school, one after school, and one on Saturday—and got a terrific turnout. Parents are clamoring for more ways to keep their middle school students on track.

◆ The eighth-grade English teachers just successfully completed a literary essay unit of study for the first time. Now they want to figure out how to get all the English teachers together to plan for how we will increase the complexity of writing from sixth to seventh to eighth grade.

- The fourth-grade teachers visited teachers at another school and came back with smart ideas about how to raise the rigor of their word study. Two of the teachers volunteered to try on the word study work and will be sharing minilessons at the next grade-level meeting.

- Our midyear assessments are showing gains in reading comprehension in our third graders. They're moving beyond the literal into interpretation, which is terrific.

- We have some dynamite teachers who are eager to share ideas with others.

What Are Some Areas of Concern with Learning and Teaching?

After hearing strengths, you will want to hear some areas of concern. I used to narrow the question to, "What are some areas of concern about literacy?" ignoring the reality that schools are organizations with interdependent relationships. While teachers may teach a particular subject or grade level, the children in the school experience all the teachers and all the grade levels. Therefore, try to determine the concerns of the whole school to get a feel for the big picture. Then you can narrow your conversation to focus on literacy.

Asking about areas of concern with learning and teaching will give you insight into what the principal considers urgent, grade levels or departments that need support in particular areas, groups of students in need of additional support, materials and resources that may be lacking, shortcomings of adult learning structures that are not working, the political context in which the school is operating, the demands of the school system, the requirements of testing and accountability, and so on.

The same group of principals listed their concerns:

- Despite our emphasis on writing in the primary grades, student writing in third through fifth grade looks like it is regressing. How can we elevate the quality of our upper-grade writing?

- We did not meet our AYP targets for some of our subgroups. We've got to figure out how to support all students.

- Even though teachers requested more grade-level planning time, they admit it is hard to stay focused and get much done.

- My fourth-grade teachers work collaboratively and there is a lot of similarity in what fourth graders are learning. But the third-grade team hasn't gelled yet and I worry that the third graders won't be adequately prepared.

- The standards tests have an abundance of informational text passages and questions but our textbook materials aren't adequate. We've got to locate supplemental materials and show teachers how to use them.

- Teachers are feeling overwhelmed. How can I be supportive yet keep the focus on the urgency of meeting students' needs?

- We just registered a large group of students from a country lacking in educational resources. What can we do to accelerate literacy learning for these older students who do not read in their native language?

- Though our emphasis is on literacy instruction, our data indicate that our students are weaker in mathematics and the district is pressuring me to shift my focus to mathematics.

 ## Understand Your Principal's Vision for Your Work

Knowing how your principal views your work and your role as a coach helps you establish a clear sense of the context in which you are working. Be it good, bad, ugly, or otherwise, you need to know where you stand. Though you may not agree with how the principal describes your role, listen to what the principal says because the perspective is likely similar to the message that the principal is communicating to teachers about coaching.

How Do You See My Role as a Coach?

Asking the principal how he or she views your role as coach can help you understand how the principal sees you interacting with teachers and students. Listen for the details such as grade level, subject, topic, specific teachers, scheduling issues, and so on, but more important, listen for the nuances in the leader's beliefs about the role of a coach. Over the past three years I have asked hundreds of literacy coaches to record their principals' answers. Here are the most frequently expressed visions of the coach's role:

Principals' Statements	My Interpretation
I've never worked with a coach before. I'm not sure what you're supposed to do.	Coach and principal will shape the coaching work together.
I'd like you to provide teachers with the support they requested to make their teaching stronger.	Coach's work needs to be aligned with teacher-identified common needs. Coach is an asset and support.
Some of my teachers just won't change their practice and I hope you'll be the one who finally motivates and gets them to do so.	Coach is seen as a "fixer of teachers," which is foreboding.
What does the district say your role is? They're the ones who told me I have to have a coach.	Coach's work will involve dismantling distrust.
I don't want to make anyone feel like they *need* a coach. I'm hoping teachers will sign up to work with you.	Coach's work should focus on those who want support. Coaching is being equated with needing remediation instead of being equated with the belief that everybody can continue to improve their practice with the support of a coach.
I'd prefer that you work with everyone on one or two grade levels so that an entire grade level benefits, rather than spread you across all grade levels where only a few on a grade level can benefit.	Coach can help build capacity within an entire grade.
I hope you can help us figure out what we can do to address the needs of certain groups of students who just aren't progressing as we hoped they would.	The coach is seen as another problem solver on the team with areas of knowledge and skill that can benefit students and teachers.

Or, your principal may have an entirely different view of your role as a coach. Listen with an open mind, ask questions, seek clarity, and reserve judgment. The point of learning about the principal's vision of coaching is not to set the principal straight, it is to understand where you stand in the principal's mind. Whether you are the first coach to coach in the school or one of many coaches with whom the principal and staff have worked, know that your role will evolve as your work unfolds during the year.

Discuss How Decisions Are Made About Which Teachers Work with the Coach

Once you have a sense of the principal's beliefs, the school's strengths and areas of need, and a beginning understanding of your role as a coach, begin to get specific about the day-to-day work. While any schedule you establish together early in the work will shift and change throughout the year as the work evolves, it is still wise to create a thoughtful plan together to begin the work.

Over time coaches should expect to work with all teachers in a variety of configurations—whole-staff professional development sessions, small-group sessions by department, grade level, or common need, one-on-one sessions in classrooms—in order to provide teachers with the support they need for their learning. In which configurations you begin working depends on the school culture and how teachers are encouraged to work with you.

Introducing the Coach

Talk with your principal about how teachers will be encouraged to begin to work with you. The goal is for you to begin to establish credibility and trusting, collaborative relationships. In some schools, literacy coaches begin with individual teachers who have expressed interest in working with a coach. In other schools, literacy coaches begin with a grade level or group of teachers who have indicated interest in participating in professional development together, frequently after engaging in careful examination of student assessment data or instructional practice and discovering a common area of need (Blachowicz, Obrochta, and Fogelberg 2005). In still others, literacy coaches begin by facilitating whole-staff professional development sessions so that everyone can check out the coach at the same time, and interested teachers can sign up for time with the coach. Given the school's culture, ask your principal what makes sense.

Build on Strengths

When I work with districts and schools that are new to coaching, I am adamant that coaches begin by working with teachers who express interest in being coached and who are eager to be coached. We want to start with positive, collaborative coaching situations so that as the teachers and the coach experience successes together, word of how terrific it is to work with a coach starts to spread, and the coach's schedule rapidly fills up. Shelley Harwayne explains, "staff development should not be perceived as something we do unto the weaker teacher or reserve for inexperienced staff members. . . . There needs to be a genuine feeling that no one has arrived. Everyone needs to be swept away by the deeply engrained value placed on adult learning" (1999, 251). I believe the same can be said for literacy coaching. We want the group of teachers we coach to include those who are perceived as already strong teachers by their colleagues so that coaching is seen as support for all teachers.

Talk with your principal about the perceptions you want to communicate about coaching. Sometimes we're not aware of the unintended messages our coaching decisions send. My colleague started coaching only the brand-new teachers to give them the support first-year teachers need at the beginning of the year. In January she had time to include more teachers on her coaching calendar and found other teachers reluctant to be coached because, inadvertently, coaching had become synonymous with something only brand-new teachers need. At another school the coach noticed that the principal sent memos that read, "Those of you who *need help*, sign up for time with the coach," to encourage interested teachers to work with the coach, but the sign-up sheet remained empty until they revised it to read, "Sign up if you are interested in working alongside the coach to meet your students' needs."

Unfortunately, in some schools literacy coaches are assigned to work with teachers who have been deemed "ineffective" during the evaluation process and are told to help improve the teacher's practice. This practice creates a toxic coaching climate across the school. The role of the coach gets intertwined with the role of the supervisor, putting both the teacher and coach in potentially adversarial positions; coaching becomes associated with remediation and not professional collaboration and inquiry; and fissures surface among members of the school community as they side with the teacher or the coach. The rationale for wanting literacy coaches to work with "ineffective" teachers is often sound and based on wanting to do as much as possible to support the teacher, and equally important, to provide the students with a solid education. But individualized coaching is not the only way you can support teachers. Brainstorm ways to support the teacher without singling out the teacher for individual "remediation" from you such as engaging the teacher in professional development with grade-level colleagues or including the teacher in group lesson-planning sessions. If your principal still insists, Cathy Toll offers helpful tips: "If a supervisor tells you that a teacher needs your help in improving performance to the satisfactory level, politely tell the supervisor that you'll wait for the teacher to approach you about the matter and then you'll be glad to help. (You may need to respectfully remind the supervisor about the need for a coach to avoid supervisory duties and point out that, if you approach the teacher, you will be acting as the representative of the supervisor)" (2004, 7).

 ## Discuss the Work You Will Do with the Whole Staff, Small Groups, Individual Teachers, or All Three

Your principal may already have a professional development plan with your role clearly defined. If so, your conversations will focus on understanding the big picture of the work and how each professional development configuration works to support the other. Or, your principal, eager to tap into your literacy knowledge, may ask for your guidance in seeing the big picture and sketching out a plan. Whether you start with your principal's plan or co-create one, a plan with a unifying focus is essential. Refer to the lists of strengths and areas of need that you created to help focus the content of the professional development.

We cannot afford to be piecemeal, scattered, or inconsistent in our work with students or with teachers if we plan to educate all students at high levels. One of your coaching roles is to help teachers connect the dots of their experiences in whole-staff or small-group sessions and in classroom coaching sessions. Discussing your principal's thoughts about the following questions can help craft your long-term and short-term professional development plan. Revisit these questions throughout the year as the focus of your professional development shifts and responds to your teachers' evolving knowledge and skills.

◆ *What may be the focus of whole-staff professional development? How often and when may we meet? To what degree does the whole-staff focus connect to the small-group and classroom coaching work?*   Whole-staff professional development sessions provide opportunities for the entire staff to work collaboratively on common goals. Everyone can hear the same message at the same time and can engage in activities that build a common conversation. Whole-staff sessions remind us to look at our work as interconnected and interdependent, to view each grade level or department not as discrete events a child experiences but as part of a unified (ideally) and cohesive whole. To give you a sense of what I mean by a whole-staff focus, here are some of the focuses in schools where I work: raising levels of student engagement, teaching reading in the content areas, using writing across the curriculum, supporting the needs of English Language Learners, employing differentiated instruction, creating and using assessment to inform instruction, and implementing standards-based lesson planning.

◆ *With which grade-level teams or small groups of teachers will I begin? How often and when may we meet?* Your school may have common planning time for teachers on a grade level or a regularly scheduled grade or department meeting. At some schools small-group sessions are convened by grade level or department because of the shared needs of students and teachers at that grade level or within that department. Find out how teachers typically use this planning or meeting time. In some districts, the collective bargaining agreement specifies how much of a teacher's planning time can be used by coaches or administrators for professional development. Be aware of those constraints as you craft a professional development plan, and be aware that as they begin to see the value of your coaching work, teachers may remove those constraints.

◆ *In which classrooms do you see me beginning to work? Which teachers at that grade level or with a similar need can attend classroom coaching sessions?* Ideally, you begin coaching in classrooms where the teacher indicates an interest in being coached. Classroom coaching is the most intensive and personalized level of support literacy coaches can provide because the coach works directly with a teacher and students. Share with the principal that how you coach does not look the same in every classroom. Knowing that the level of support in classroom coaching varies from demonstrating lessons, to side-by-side teaching, to observing lessons and offering feedback helps the principal talk to teachers about your role and may get teachers interested in working with you.

Explain to the principal that you would like to build a collaborative classroom coaching culture not only between you and individual teachers but also among teachers. When you work in classrooms, you would like to have at least one teacher—if not a number of others—observing and participating in the work. That way, when you leave the teacher after your work together, the observing teachers go back and try what the coach demonstrated in their colleague's classroom right away and the teacher has colleagues with whom to discuss the work. Conversations and collaboration with colleagues helps the coaching work take hold and flourish and helps build capacity across a group of teachers, not just one teacher at a time.

Who Will Teach the Students When Teachers Participate in Professional Development Opportunities During the School Day?

Now might be a good time to talk with your principal about the feasibility of creating opportunities for teachers to collaborate. The answer to the question of freeing up teacher time is rarely easy and usually requires creative thinking and reallocation of resources. Strategies for freeing up teachers to participate in professional development opportunities during the school day include:

◆ *Your school or district provides job-embedded professional development time. Some schools or districts build professional development time into the school day, providing teachers with a set number of minutes per day, week, or month to engage in ongoing professional development opportunities while school is in session.* Even with the allocated time, you may have to do some juggling. For example, if all your sixth-grade literacy teachers share the same common planning time while the sixth graders are in mathematics class, working together as a team in a sixth-grade literacy classroom with students will require adjusting the schedule. Perhaps the literacy teacher with whom you want to work can juggle her schedule with the mathematics teacher so that her students are available during the period when the team of teachers can observe.

◆ *Your school has some discretionary funds that can be spent on coverage.* Are funds available for hiring substitute teachers to provide coverage on days in which teachers need to collaborate? Even better, is there a way your principal can hire a part-time teacher who can teach students on a regular basis while teachers engage in professional development? One school where I work hired a chorus teacher two days a week. Each grade level has chorus once a week to create time for literacy teachers to work together. Another school hired a retired reading teacher who brought two classes together into the school library and read aloud to them while their teachers collaborated.

◆ *Your teachers are willing to establish structures that allow collaboration.* In my school, we all established reading buddies. Each upper-grade class paired up with a lower-grade class and, on a regular basis, the two classes met to read together. When I needed to collaborate with my grade-level colleagues or attend a professional development opportunity during the school day and no substitute coverage could be provided, I asked my reading buddy colleague if she would be willing to bring both classes together for reading buddies so that I could attend the session. I returned the favor when she wanted to attend a session with her grade level.

◆ *Your administrators teach small and large groups of students.* One middle school principal I know teaches "college class" each week. During college class, he gathers and teaches an entire grade level for an hour in the auditorium while their teachers participate in professional development sessions led by the literacy coach.

Establish Regular Communication

Knowing that your regular meeting time is bound to get rescheduled and shuffled around, strive to set a regular meeting time so that you have time to collaborate, reflect on the work, and plan next steps. Your meeting time might involve planning upcoming professional development or reflecting on the most recent sessions. You might schedule time to observe classroom practice together to identify patterns and trends, or your principal might observe you leading professional development sessions or engaged in classroom coaching in order to give you feedback on your work.

Keep the Principal Informed of Your Work

Keeping the principal informed about coaching work is essential and is a rich learning opportunity for the principal. Encourage the principal to attend grade-level meetings to be a part of the work. Keep your principal informed of your schedule. My principal used to stop by for a few minutes during our grade-level meetings, providing us with an opportunity to ask her questions, request additional supports, and share our work. Often she would follow up with me later in the day to make sure the team felt supported and had what we needed to move forward in our work. When she could not attend, I wrote a quick note to keep her abreast of our work (see Figure 3–1). I also emailed copies of the note to the teachers who attended the meeting to ease any potential distrust of the intent of my communication with the principal.

Invite the Principal to Observe Coaching

Demonstration lessons provide an ideal opportunity for the principal to see the coach in action. As the coaching work moves away from the coach demonstrating lessons, to the coach and teacher working side-by-side, to the teacher taking on most of the work, be honest about the additional level of pressure the principal's presence can put on a teacher. Some teachers crave

5/18
To: Anna Marie
From: Katherine
Re: Fourth-Grade Literacy Planning

I met with the fourth-grade team on Monday and we discussed a number of important literacy issues including preparing our students for the rigors of standards testing in an organized, purposeful fashion from the first day of school. All the teachers reported that they have a multitude of resources including lots of supplementary texts to use for reading and writing minilessons and test-prep materials. *However, they need time to plan out the entire literacy year together*.

I think that mapping out the year on a monthly and then weekly basis would be *very* powerful. I could help the team figure out which texts to use that either connect directly with the units being taught or help reinforce concepts that need to be covered for the standards tests. I could also help the team figure out how to prepare students for the language of testing (such as "in which passage is this statement not false?").

This is what I'd like to propose, and please let me know whether it is feasible:

1. Ask the team to sort through their materials and organize materials by unit in advance.
2. Meet as a team in June for a half-day of planning (from 12:00 to 3:00) with coverage provided for all four teachers and me.
3. If you can give us the half-day together, everyone on the team agreed to "donate" two hours from 3:00 to 5:00 so that we can spend a solid five hours on the work.

Is this possible? Could we have a half-day in June? Does this make sense? Thank you for your feedback and consideration.

FIG. 3–1 Keep the principal informed

an audience. Others need the security of trying on work without the principal in the room. As the teachers you coach become more confident about their work, suggest inviting the principal in to see the growth in the students and to celebrate the teacher's accomplishments. The more often the principal is a part of the coaching work, the less intimidating and more collaborative observations can become.

Inform the Principal's Observation of Instruction

Though the responsibility of teacher evaluation lies with the principal or vice-principal, coaches should keep administrators informed about the coaching work so that teachers are fairly evaluated. Share the focus of the coaching work. Describe what the administrator can expect to see in classrooms. If the administrator attends demonstration lessons and participates in ongoing professional development opportunities you lead, use those experiences as examples. Explain what is not yet happening in classrooms and be ready to provide a time line for when those changes can be expected. If you put the information in writing, as shown in Figure 3–2, share it with the teacher first to make sure the content is accurate, and give a copy to the teacher.

Discuss How to Improve Your Work

Be ready to have your work analyzed and evaluated. Since the coach is responsible for improving teacher practice to improve student learning, whenever a teacher with whom the coach has been working for some time is observed, it is an evaluation of the coach's work with that teacher. My principal used to ask me, "What evidence of your coaching work should I see when I observe the teacher and students?" She firmly believed that if she could not tell I had worked with a teacher based on what the students and teacher now knew how to do, I was not adding value. After observing teachers' lessons, I knew my principal would meet with me first to discuss what more I needed to do as a coach to support the teachers with whom I worked. Whether or not your principal gives you suggestions about how to improve your work, analyzing your own coaching work with the question, What evidence of my coaching work should I see in the teacher and students? helps you gauge and modify your coaching to improve teaching and learning.

3/11
To: Rebecca (principal)
From: Katherine (school-based coach)
Re: Adrianne's upcoming lesson
Cc: Adrianne

Hi Rebecca,

Adrianne let me know you've scheduled an observation in her class-room this Friday. She's excited to show you what we've been working on to raise the level of participation of her reluctant speakers during class discussions.

I'd like to remind you of the work Adrianne and I have been doing together during the past two weeks. During the demonstration lesson you observed last Monday, you saw how I charted three of the guiding questions that we would be discussing during the read aloud (To what degree are these characters believable? Whose voices are being heard? Whose voices are missing?). Adrianne is finding that when she charts the guiding questions and refers to them throughout the read-aloud, more students engage in quality partner talk. Please look for the guiding questions when you observe her lesson. You might also look at the whiteboard behind the classroom library to see charts of the various questions she has used during the past two weeks. Remember when Adrianne asked at the grade-level meeting why we are encouraging teachers to leave up charts? Yesterday she remarked that her students are actually using those questions as they partner talk about their independent reading! She's seeing the value of leaving up charts!

You may also see students jotting ideas down on index cards during the read-aloud. Adrianne and I gathered a group of her students who don't usually talk during whole-class lessons and asked them what they need from us to participate more. The majority mentioned that conversation moves too quickly for them and that they need time to jot down ideas before talking. Adrianne has practiced giving students time to stop and jot before talking.

Now that more students are participating, Adrianne and I are starting to deal with the challenge of how to hear all of their voices and how to build stronger conversation. You may observe students stating good ideas and Adrianne not sure what to do with some of the comments that seem different from others. We're working on that next week. Please let me know what additional supports you believe Adrianne's students need so that we can incorporate those into our work together.

FIG. 3–2 Let the principal know what to look for

Relationships, Relationships, Relationships

When I first started coaching, I had no idea what to talk about with my principal and we plugged along, figuring it out together. When I started coaching in a new district without already established relationships, in schools where the principals expected me to show them how to use a coach, I scrambled to figure out what to even talk about. This chapter covers quite a bit of ground to give you ideas about the types of conversations you can have with your principal. You, too, will plug along with your principal as you solidify clear boundaries and establish an effective relationship. Yes, I'm starting to sound like a broken record, but I'll say it again: Literacy coaching is all about relationships. Now let's shift our attention to how to determine teacher strengths and areas of need to inform your coaching relationship.

Getting Started
Teacher Strengths and Needs

Teachers use a variety of methods to gather information about what their students know about literacy and how they learn: running records, writing samples, portfolios, student self-assessments and goal setting, conversations with students, formal classroom observations, conferring notes, anecdotal records, informal and formal assessments, and listening to student conversations.

Likewise, literacy coaches can use a variety of methods to gather information about their teachers' content knowledge, pedagogical knowledge, and learning styles. To repeat: the purpose of gathering information and creating theories about teachers' strengths and areas of need is not to judge or rank a teacher, but rather to determine what teachers need next for their learning, decide how to best support them, and make sure the ongoing professional development increases student learning. Only when literacy coaches base their professional development planning on the expressed or assessed needs of their teachers and students will professional development sessions be most effective.

If you're a coach, you probably work with teachers in a variety of structured settings, from whole-staff professional development sessions to small-group or grade-level sessions, to individualized coaching sessions. Making decisions about with whom to work in which structure involves analyzing teachers' content and pedagogical knowledge and skill as well as understanding how each teacher learns best.

To establish a rationale for coaching in general and for learning about teachers' strengths and areas of need in particular, I often begin my coaching work with a group activity designed to help us all become aware of what is involved with learning. I ask everyone to think about something they learned to do, like cooking, playing a sport, learning a language, and so on. Then I think aloud about when I learned to practice yoga. I attended classes for "brand-new beginners" after discovering the beginner class was too challenging. My teacher, Amy, explained everything, demonstrated the different poses repeatedly, told us which mats, blocks, and straps to purchase, and gave us time to practice. When Amy realized I couldn't follow her oral directions, she adjusted my body, helping me do things I couldn't believe I could do. She made our mistakes fun by having us practice falling over, showing us how she struggled with some poses, and explaining that some things would take years of practice to be able to do. Amy even asked us all to share what we hoped to get out of yoga and a bit about our athletic histories. She adjusted her pacing based on us, gave us things to practice between classes, and cautioned us about trying on too much too soon. Repetition, responsiveness, patience, and exemplary modeling were the hallmarks of her class.

After participants quietly brainstorm what was involved in their own learning experience, I have them write a list of what they needed to be successful, and then as a group we share the characteristics of our learning experiences. We notice that whether we learned to practice yoga, cook, drive, play tennis, or install a sprinkler system, we all requested repeated demonstrations and explanations from someone knowledgeable and skilled in what we were learning to do. Encouraging words, clear guidance, and opportunities to approximate without fear of humiliation helped us past our own insecurities and awkward first attempts. Some of us needed hands-on guidance, while others relied on visuals, and still others wanted to practice alone for a bit and then wanted more instruction. As we discuss the similarities in our experiences, I highlight how much our teachers based their teaching decisions on what we needed for our learning. And I explain why, as a literacy coach, I believe it is essential to gather information in a variety of ways so that we can be successful at supporting learning.

Gather Information

There are many ways to gather information about teachers' strengths and needs.

One-on-One Conversations with the Teacher

Try having a one-on-one conversation with your teachers after they reflect on a time when they learned to do something well. Ask them:

◆ What do you believe are your strengths as a teacher? Or, to make it more specific, you could ask, What do you believe are your strengths as a teacher of reading? writing?

◆ What are your areas of need as a teacher?

◆ What supports do you need for your learning? How do you learn best? (Think back to our conversations about something each of us learned to do.)

After a few conversations, you will start to notice patterns. Figure 4–1 shows a spreadsheet I created from a handful of one-on-one conversations with teachers. The teachers gave me clues into what they need for their learning and how they learn—viewing lessons, co-planning time, research, high-interest materials, strategies to support a wide range of students, ways to get students involved and interested. I need to keep in mind that these conversations are only one source of information and, just as a teacher does not base her understanding of a student on one assessment, neither can I. But these conversations can help me begin to shape my understanding of each teacher as a learner and some of each teacher's beliefs about teaching and learning. From this I can begin to form my professional development decisions of *what* I may teach and *how* I may teach it.

Analyzing the spreadsheet, I can already see that my coaching work will involve demonstrating lessons because the majority want to see the work in action. I'll need to choose structures that involve watching and analyzing lessons. I also know teachers want and need time to plan with colleagues, so I'll include planning time within my sessions.

The sheet also reveals teachers' beliefs about homogeneous grouping; the need for scripted curriculum materials; attitudes about the lack of parent involvement; and some blame-the-student issues. As I craft my coaching work, I'll need to determine how to address these beliefs and attitudes. The tricky part about beliefs is that our experiences shape and reinforce them, and they, in turn, support or hinder the development of our skills. When I didn't know how to teach upper elementary students how to read, I started to believe that upper elementary students cannot learn how to read. Luckily, I worked with educators who helped me translate statements such as "I don't think these students can learn to read" into an awareness that I didn't know how to teach upper-grade students to read, and intervened with effective professional development. Talking and reading about how to work with upper-grade readers didn't shift my beliefs. Sure, I listened when colleagues

Teacher	Strengths—What are your strengths as a teacher?	Needs—What are your areas of need as a teacher?	Supports—How can we support your learning?	Action Plan, Theory, or Wonderings
Anita	I care about kids; I try on new ideas that research says work. I plan solid lessons if I have enough time.	I don't have enough texts that my students like to read; finding time to plan is hard with all of the challenges of the school day.	More materials; more time to plan on my own; I need to see what more effective lessons look like.	*Make sure to have research available for Anita* *See it*
Brad	I love teaching; the students keep me energized, especially when I can see the lightbulbs going off.	It is really hard to work with such a diverse group of students; prefer homogeneous grouping.	Consider regrouping classes back to homogeneous class structure; show me what works with my students.	*Differentiated instruction strategies?* *See it*
Carmen	I try to give my students authentic tasks that lead toward independence. Preparing them for the world is so important to me.	I need help planning lessons that get students excited. When they're interested in the topic, they're excited.	More planning time with colleagues; maybe co-planning lessons would help.	*Engagement strategies?* *Co-planning*
Diana	I know my content area. I've taught writing for years and students love what we do.	I need more time with my students because they're pretty far behind. How do I get them caught up?	Not sure.	*Accelerated learning strategies?*
Elizabeth	Reading lots of adolescent texts to connect my students to books.	More involved parents because students aren't doing their homework.	Someone who can show me how to get struggling students to do their work; I need to see things working with my students.	*Strategies for struggling students?* *How is "struggling" being defined?* *See it* *Continues*

FIG. 4–1 Teaching staff at a glance

Teacher	Strengths— What are your strengths as a teacher?	Needs—What are your areas of need as a teacher?	Supports— How can we support your learning?	Action Plan, Theory, or Wonderings
Fran	Teaching writing is my passion. I spend a lot of time planning my reading lessons.	Better curriculum guide so planning doesn't take so long since I've got young children at home.	More planning time or a better curriculum guide; demos in my classroom don't help me because I get distracted by student behaviors. But I'd like to participate in my colleagues' rooms.	*Not sure— gather more info about what is taking time in her planning?* *Planning*
Gordon	Working to figure out how to support my students' needs while trying to raise the bar.	Not sure how to address standards when my students are so low.	Demonstration lessons with *my* kind of students.	*Supporting students? Accelerating students?* *See it*
Hector	Plan with my colleagues so we're on the same page.	Conferring— how to keep track of student information.	Strategies for keeping track of student info and ways to use the info for lesson planning; confer- ring in my room would be helpful.	*Conferring? Strategies for using student info in lesson planning?* *See it*
Isobel	I base my lessons on my students' needs and standards.	Students need to be more motivated.	Motivation strategies— maybe a demo in my class?	*Engagement strategies?* *See it*
Julia	Students really learn from me.	I think we need a better spelling program since student writing shows lots of spelling errors.	Not sure.	*Not sure— gather more info*

FIG. 4–1 Cont.

assured me that my students could learn to read, I read the professional texts, and I acknowledged that students in other classrooms were learning, but I didn't really believe *my* students could until my literacy coach joined me in my classroom and *showed* me how to teach my students to read. As I gained the knowledge and skills to teach reading and achieved successes with my struggling readers, my beliefs shifted.

Your coaching work will certainly address teachers' beliefs, sometimes by discussing them, sometimes by reading professional texts that challenge them, but most often by working alongside teachers to help them gain the knowledge and skill that ultimately shift their beliefs. "Students need to be more motivated" translates to showing teachers how to motivate and engage their students. "I need demonstrations with *my* kind of students" translates to working with this teacher in the classroom to *show* him how to meet *all* students' needs. And "I prefer homogeneous grouping" translates to showing the teacher how to differentiate instruction to provide access for a wide range of learners.

Observations of Teachers During Professional Development Sessions

How teachers engage in professional development sessions can also help you get to know teachers as learners. Pay attention to how your teachers participate in professional development sessions. As a keen observer of adult learners, you can use the information you gather to help you create more supportive professional development sessions. For example, if you observe that teachers have ah-ha moments after analyzing student work together, ask them what made the experience enlightening. If you observe teachers tuning out during a professional text discussion, try to figure out why so that the next time you discuss a professional text you can do so in a more engaging manner. Some questions to consider:

◆ What is the teacher's level of participation during professional development?

◆ Which aspects of the sessions seem to engage and disengage the teacher?

◆ What questions or concerns does the teacher raise?

◆ What requests does the teacher make for additional learning experiences?

◆ What does the teacher's exit slip reveal?

◆ After the session, to what degree does the teacher utilize new learning in her/his teaching?

Analysis of a Variety of Student Data

Student data, both hard data—such as standardized test and standards-based test scores—and soft data—such as student work samples, running records, conferring notes, and portfolios—can provide you with useful information.

Using Test Scores to Help Uncover Strengths and Areas of Need

I have mixed feelings about the efficacy of standardized and standards-based tests to reveal accurate information about student achievement. Nevertheless, testing is a powerful and, for many students, life-altering reality. As Harvey Daniels (2005) writes, "If politicians and the public think the tests are fair enough, and if life's opportunities will be dealt out to children based on these scores, then we teachers have to pitch in and close the gap."

When I was a teacher, my principal used the breakdown of my students' annual standardized test scores to reveal what I needed to do to close the gap in my teaching. We compared my students' scores from the previous year with the scores they received after a year with me, and noted whether they made progress. We scrutinized the summary sheet that broke the total reading and writing score into multiple subscores, each aligned with a particular standard. We looked further to see on which aspects of reading and writing my students scored high or low. I discovered that my students scored higher on fictional passages than they did on informational text passages, which should not have surprised me as much as it did, given that I mostly focused on reading fiction. Our close look at the test data helped me realize that I did not know much about teaching informational text reading, that my classroom library lacked engaging informational texts students could actually read, and that I needed to figure out how to teach informational text reading because my students were being shortchanged.

We also compared the previous year's scores to the current year's scores and found that students who were already scoring high kept scoring high. Students who scored lowest the previous year had noticeably improved, thanks in part to my participation in grade-level sessions that focused directly on how to support at-risk readers. But the students in the middle—students who completed their reading and writing work quietly or who came into the fourth grade reading transitional chapter books such as Bailey School Kids books, The Magic Tree House books, The Littles, and so on, fell behind. Again, my principal and I talked about what could be causing those students to slip, and realized that because the students were reading fairly well, enjoyed reading, and did so without much fanfare or need for my attention, they were slipping below my radar screen. My principal asked if I knew how to move the students out of transitional reading and into self-extending reading (Fountas and Pinnell, 2000), and I admitted I did not really know what to do for those students beyond what I was already doing.

As we engaged in our data-based conversation, my emotions ranged from guilt that I did not do enough for my students, to fear that my principal would think less of me as a teacher and possibly note as much in my file, to curiosity about what more I could do as a teacher to improve my craft. But my principal's purpose wasn't to play a gotcha game or to write me up. Instead, she maintained an investigative stance: she wanted to figure out what more her students and their teacher needed for their learning so that she could gather resources to address the gaps in my teaching. After similar conversations with my colleagues, my principal determined that I was not alone in my need for more work on reading informational texts and meeting the needs of transitional readers. Soon study groups formed, led by colleagues who had strengths in each area, and professional development sessions occurred, led by a district coach, and we all improved our teaching practices.

As a literacy coach, you may not have access to individual students' test score information, nor may you want to begin early in your coaching work by sitting down with a teacher to engage in the type of conversation my principal had with me, since you are still working on building trust. But know that because one of your roles, according to the International Reading Association (2006), is to be a "skillful evaluator of literacy needs," you need to develop your ability to analyze and communicate with teachers about student data. Often included in the testing results schools receive are summary scores for the entire school and for each grade level. Ask your principal if you can look at the summary sheets of data broken down by grade level or by standard or subgroup to uncover areas of strength and need. Learn as much as you can about what is tested on each test and how so that you are informed. Download released test items and analyze the layout, format, and types of questions and prompts. Read everything posted on the district website about the assessments. The more you know about tests, the better you can become at analyzing the data and creating hypotheses about what students and teachers may need next for their learning. Then you can start brainstorming ways you can help support teachers in strengthening the areas of need.

Use "Soft Data" to Get to Know Your Teachers

Much happens in classrooms that can help you get to know your teachers. Who uses conferring notes well to shape writing instruction? Which students are writing breathtaking poetry, memoirs, informational texts, or narratives? Which classes have lively discussions about a wide variety of genres and authors? Which displays of student work are evolving and changing to reflect increased student knowledge and skill? Who is reaching at-risk students? Look at student work, classroom environments, and published writing; watch and listen to students at work; marvel at the talents of your teachers and note their strengths. As your coaching work evolves and you work to build capacity, you will want to tap into the existing strengths teachers reveal in their day-to-day work.

 ## Trends and Patterns

The purpose of using various sources of information such as meeting with the principal, having one-on-one conversations with teachers, observing teachers in professional development sessions, analyzing hard and soft data is to help determine the trends and patterns in *what* teachers need for their learning—and what kind of learners the teachers are—to best shape *how* those needs should be met using many possible professional development structures as described in Part II. Determining trends and patterns will help you decide what to study with the whole staff, in small groups, and with individual teachers in their classrooms.

 ## Taking a Closer Look—Beginning a Classroom Coaching Relationship

One of your coaching responsibilities may be to coach teachers in their classrooms, which is the most intense level of support you can provide because it involves working directly with teachers and their students. To begin your classroom coaching work with a teacher, you'll need more than just methods of getting to know teachers. You'll want to gather as much specific information as you can about the teacher and students. The information you gather should relate to professional development focus you and your principal may have already discussed together and to what the teacher has identified as an area of concern. For example, if you're to coach in the realm of writing workshop, your initial data gathering should be on writing.

First Conversations

All coaching is individualized; there is not one specific structure, model, or script. What follows are suggestions for what to discuss during your first conversations with a teacher with whom you plan to have a classroom coaching relationship, meaning you plan to work side-by-side with the teacher and her students. They are meant as guidelines for the information you'll want to gather to help shape your coaching decisions. Whenever possible, have your conversation in the teacher's classroom so that you can look at the classroom environment (this is a perfect time to ask if you can copy down or take photos of charts and other visuals or physical arrangements that support learning) and so that the students' work is immediately accessible during your conversation. Be ready to take notes so that you can capture the ideas that you discuss.

Discuss Students' Strengths and Needs ◆ Set up a meeting with the teacher to explain why you want to know more about his students. I usually say, "I'm really excited about working with you and your students. I'd like to know as much as I can about them so that I can plan lessons with you that are based on your students' needs. What can you share with me about your students? Also, you'll notice I brought my computer. May I please take notes as you talk so that I can remember what we've discussed? I'll email you a copy of my notes to add to your anecdotal records, since we'll be discussing information about your students you may find helpful." With the teacher, look at various sources of data including:

- ◆ Standards assessment data
- ◆ Standardized test data
- ◆ Classroom assessments
- ◆ The teacher's anecdotal records such as conferring notes, observation notes, or anecdotal records
- ◆ Student work

Ask the teacher to identify and discuss students who are doing particularly well or who are concerning her. Some teachers feel more comfortable talking about students who are doing well while others feel more comfortable talking about students who are concerning them. Listen and take notes as the teacher talks, and begin to analyze the teacher's comments. How we talk about our students often reveals what we are focused on in our teaching. Is the teacher focused on behavior and management issues? Listen with an ear for understanding, which means don't judge, but to try to get a comprehensive understanding of the classroom dynamics.

After the meeting, reread your notes and form some initial theories about what students need for their learning. Highlight the names of any students who interest you, and jot down reminders of what to look for when you observe. A thoughtful meeting with a teacher can help shape how you observe—which students to watch, classroom dynamics, teacher-student and student-student interactions—and help you refine your theories.

Figure 4–2 shows some information I gathered from a meeting with Alexandra, a seventh-grade teacher I began working with during the fourth week of school. It includes a transcript of the teacher's words and my notes so that you can see how I am listening for strengths to confirm, students to watch, questions to consider further. In Figure 4–3, I start to form ideas for my first classroom observation using an observation planning sheet I created.

Teacher's words	My notes
My students and I have built a strong classroom community really quickly and I feel like I know a lot about them because I did informal reading interviews with each student. I also had students write about their lives as writers and readers. According to the standards testing, the majority of my class scored at the basic level in reading and writing (one level below meeting standards), so the majority are not meeting standards yet. You might think my students are English Learners because 98 percent are of Mexican descent, but actually only one-third speak Spanish as their first language. Of the eleven who are English Learners, four did not make progress last year on their English Language development assessment. I think motivation is an issue for some of my students like Javier, Mercedes, Miguel, and Angelina because I can't seem to get them involved in lessons. And what do I do about the students like Cesar, Lizabet, Sintia, Mario, and Jose P., who participate actively in writing and reading minilessons, read-alouds, and shared readings, but don't seem to transfer that knowledge and skill to their independent reading and writing?	Strong community! Wants to get to know her students and knows quite a bit already. What did she learn about students from informal interviews? How is info informing instructional decisions? Check disaggregated test data— Are there obvious areas of weakness? Which English Language Learners are languishing? Keep an eye on "unmotivated" students. What supports is the teacher providing? Perhaps gradual release isn't as strong as it needs to be for students?

FIG. 4–2 Discussing student strengths and needs with a teacher

Teacher _Alexandra_	**Grade** _7th_	**Date** _10/3_

Lesson focus: (What are students expected to know and be able to do as a result of the lesson?)

Students to focus on:	**My notes**
Javier—Motivation?	
Mercedes—Motivation?	
Miguel—Motivation?	
Angelina—Motivation?	

Classroom environment to focus on:	
Strong community	

Pedagogy to focus on:	
What are students expected to know and be able to do as a result of the lesson?	
Supports for English Learners—How is she providing scaffolds for English Learners?	
Questioning strategies	
Use of think-aloud	

Continues

FIG. 4–3 Observation planning sheet

Classroom Routines:

Signal for silence	Transitions	Seating arrangements (student-selected, seating plan?)
How students keep track of their learning? (notebooks, take notes?)	How do students get to share thinking and work? (bring a few kids up, share in partnerships, called on one at a time?)	How do students formalize or generalize their learning for the day? (In writing, with partners, as a class?)

Other notes:

_____

_____

_____

_____

FIG. 4–3 Cont.

You'll notice that my sheet includes space to take notes on students. One way I build trust with teachers is to pay attention during lessons to any students they discuss with me earlier. After the lesson teachers frequently remark, "Thanks for actually paying attention to the students I mentioned before." I take notes on the classroom environment, so that I can compare my impressions with the teacher's, and usually on the teacher's pedagogy. And, because my coaching work involves demonstrating lessons, I take notes on the routines so that when I teach, I can utilize already-established procedures.

Discuss the Teacher's Strengths and Needs ◆ From your conversation, you'll hear snippets of information indicating what the teacher considers are her strengths and areas of need. Ask the teacher to talk about what the class has been studying and working on lately. Guide your conversation to get a sense of what is going well and what may be troubling the teacher. If the teacher seems to focus on what isn't working, ask about successes. If everything seems amazing, ask about areas of concern. A conversation with a teacher is like any other conversation—you'll have to make decisions about what to ask, how to ask, and when to ask based on the teacher's personality, comfort level with you, and so on. Learning from the teacher about the teacher is essential. We all want to be heard. Having a stranger come into your classroom to work with you on things you didn't even say you want or need is not a promising start to a coaching relationship. Craft your own way of asking, "What do you believe is important for us to work on together?" Again, take notes as you talk. The teacher's response may be vague ("Whatever you think we should work on"), or challenging ("I don't know why I have to work with you, anyway"), or specific ("No matter how hard I try, my students want to go from drafting to final publication without revision. Can you help me teach revision strategies better?") Every response is revealing and will help you work with the teacher.

Figure 4–4 is another excerpt of my conversation with Alexandra as we discussed her strengths and needs. As I reread my notes, I see that I have some wonderings that may be addressed in the short term and others that will shape our work in the long term.

Find out how the teacher feels comfortable learning—through viewing lessons, professional reading and application, co-planning, side-by-side teaching, watching and analyzing instructional videos, observing lessons in another teacher's classroom, lesson study, observation and feedback—and figure out why. I usually say something like, "We're going to have an opportunity to work together in your classroom with your students. To make my work with you and your students stronger, I'd like to know how you see our work together." You may want to ask the teacher what has worked in the past and what hasn't. Again, take as many notes as you can so that you can develop an understanding of the teacher as a learner. In my experience, teachers usually choose viewing lessons, observation with feedback, and professional reading as ways they learn best because those are more familiar structures than side-by-side coaching. Keep in mind that you are at the beginning of what will be an ongoing relationship and there will be time to introduce the teacher to other ways of you can work together. Alexandra's comments helped me determine how to support her learning (see Figure 4–5).

Teacher's words	My notes
I'm so nervous about you watching me teach! What if my lesson totally bombs? OK, so what's going well? When I used the shared reading approach to teach my reading lessons I feel like my students are really with me, involved, and learning. Their ability to talk about the meaning of the text is improving. But when I do a read-aloud, I think I'm losing the students. I don't really know how to figure out if they're listening and getting what I want them to know and be able to do.	Shared reading—feels more confident. What is she doing in shared reading that could be applied to read-aloud? Meaning making—what does she think are the big ideas in the texts?
I've been working on using higher-level questions since my department is trying to increase the rigor in what we're doing. We noticed last year that all of us teachers tend to ask lots of literal questions. But I think my questions might be too hard for the students because they don't really know the answers.	Focused on questioning strategies. Is she modeling answering strategies, too? Are questions charted as a visual support for students?
Something that confuses me is knowing when to think aloud and how often.	Watch for think-aloud
And how am I supposed to figure out which standards to address in lessons when I've got students below, at, and above grade level in my class?	Address the role of standards at some point

FIG. 4–4 Discussing teacher strengths and needs with a teacher

As your first planning conversation comes to an end, it is helpful to summarize what you've learned about the students and the teacher and to explain the purpose of your observation. This allows you to check your understanding with the teacher's, to revise your notes, to continue to establish trust, and to allow the teacher more time to ask you questions.

Here's a portion of what I said to Alexandra at the end of our first meeting:

I'm excited to see the classroom community you've built with your students. I'm going to pay special attention to the students you mentioned—Javier, Mercedes, Miguel, and Angelina—who seem to lack motivation, so that we can problem-solve strategies for working with them. I admire your willingness to have me observe a read-aloud since

Teacher's words	My notes
How can you support me? BE HONEST. I want to know how to improve my instruction and it bothers me when people start with the positives. I know the other shoe is going to drop, so just tell me what I need to help my students learn.	Honest feedback
I've seen a few demonstration lessons and those are helpful. But you know what gets in my way? I know I should do things differently as I teach, but it feels like my teaching is a habit and it is hard to change what I do. Maybe you could help me during the lesson? But I'm not sure how that would work.	Possible side-by-side coaching model? Be prepared to demonstrate suggestions
Don't give me lots of things to work on at one time. I'll tell you that I can take on the world, but I know that I'll get frustrated.	Narrow focus
Really, I want you to be honest. No sugar-coating the truth. But if you think I should do something differently, I'm going to ask you to show me how with my students so I can figure out what you're talking about.	

FIG. 4–5 Brainstorming teacher supports

you're not feeling as confident with that approach. I'll be paying attention to a few things as you teach—the students you mentioned, your questioning strategies since that's the focus of your department's work, and how engaged students seem to be in the read-aloud since you're worried about that. I'm also curious about what it may take to address the needs of the English Learners who didn't seem to make enough growth last year, so I'll see how you're trying to support them during the lesson. What are the four students' names? I've put in my notes that the issue of standards and how to transfer the knowledge and skill students seem to demonstrate in lessons into their independent reading and writing as things we'll want to figure out together in our work. Do you have any questions of me or anything else you'd like to add?

Ask the teacher where she would feel comfortable having you sit during the observation. Unless the teacher has another preference, you may want to ask if you can sit as close to the students as possible so that you can hear their thoughts and ideas.

After the meeting, take some time to gather your thoughts and to plan for your observation. You may want to review your notes and add any additional thoughts to the first observation planning sheet. If your note taking is worrying the teacher, offer to email or give a copy of your notes to him. Remember, you're building trust.

A Note About Note Taking

Some teachers equate note taking with evaluation because their only experience with having a visitor in the room is when the principal conducts a formal evaluation. Since evaluation is the role of the principal and not the role of the coach, and since note taking is equated with evaluation, teachers may expect that coaches won't be taking notes. Wrong! Coaches must write down what students and teachers are saying and doing so that they can have evidence-based discussions. Your conversations cannot be limited to what you remember happening, which becomes blurred by your judgments almost immediately. As the doors to classrooms open up and more educators spend time in each other's rooms, teachers will become more comfortable with people observing them, taking notes to remember what is happening in the lesson, what students are saying and doing, and what the teacher is saying and doing.

The notes I take are informative, not evaluative. And there is a big difference. Evaluative notes are often vague and laced with opinions. Informative notes script, as close to verbatim as possible, what the teacher and students say and do. The purpose of informative notes is to help both you and the teacher get as clear a picture as possible about what happens during a lesson so that you can analyze the lesson and make decisions about what needs to happen in the next lesson. Informative notes are an ongoing record that helps direct your work. Figure 4–6 is an example of the difference between informative and evaluative notes. If you don't feel comfortable showing the notes you take to the teacher, they're probably more evaluative than informative.

Topics in a Coach's Notes

My laptop is always with me when I'm coaching. I type everything I can capture. Your coaching notes will include:

- what teachers say and do during lessons

- what students say and do during lessons

- what gets recorded on charts

- your impressions (*This question got kids animated! And Annalisa finally spoke during the lesson!*)

Informative	Evaluative
9:12 a.m. Began by reviewing the chart from yesterday *Expectations for "Accountable Talk"* • *Think* • *Talk* • *Share* • *Make connections* *Ask yourself: What's going on?* *What am I learning about the characters* *through their:* • *Actions (the way they act)* • *Words (what they say)* Reminded students of yesterday's work— *We practiced turning and talking, getting* *our ideas heard by our classmates.* *Remember to share out loud so that we* *can hear your smart thinking.* *The whole time I'm reading I want you to* *think, "What's going on?" Let's practice* *by turning to our partners.* Back to the circle 9:15 *Thank you, Mr. Falker* written by Patricia Polacco Walked around to show students the first page and how the words are italicized. *What does it mean when an author uses* *italics?* Student—important words! Slanted words are important words!	9:12 a.m. Began by reviewing the chart from yesterday. T—Set the purpose for the lesson. *Do you remember the chart?* S—Most students nodded. Good pacing. Got into reading the book right away. Showed students the first page and explained the role of italics. 9:15 Read first page with expression. Could go slower for second- language learners? Turn and talk—2 minutes. Got to 8 out of 30 students. What about the rest? Two students off task. 9:20 Back as a group. Asked students to shared idea. Couldn't hear students. *Continues*

FIG. 4–6 Informative versus evaluative notes

Informative	Evaluative
Teacher—*That's right. The message must be really important if the author italicized the words. Let's figure out the importance of the message.*	
9:16 Read the first page to students *Think about the message—Turn and talk—Why did the grandpa put honey on the book?*	
9:18 Walked around the circle and stopped at Julio and Fernando. Prompted student to ask another question.	
9:20 Brought students back together as a group. *Who wants to share the author's message so far?*	

FIG. 4–6 Cont.

- ◆ your ideas for next steps (*Keep using the chart—kids referred to it repeatedly; maybe another Eve Bunting book to build ideas?*)

- ◆ what you need to learn more about (*More strategies for language development?* or *What revision minilessons are working for other teachers on this grade?*)

- ◆ possible resources to gather for the teacher (*Needs more persuasive mentor texts. Find fifth-grade writing samples to show fourth-grade teachers where students are headed.*)

- ◆ notes about ideas to share with other teachers (*Tell other seventh-grade teachers that their idea about co-constructed charts worked!*)

- ◆ notes for your preconference and post conference

- ◆ notes you take during conferences

My notes help me have accountable conversations with teachers because I can cite evidence of what happened in lessons, what we discussed in prior meetings together, and use them to help me remember and follow through with things I said I'd do for the teacher. My note-taking habit makes some people uncomfortable at first because they distrust the content ("you're writing down everything I'm bad at") or my motives ("you're going to use the notes against me, maybe share them with the principal"). Emailing notes to teachers as a recap of the coaching work helps ameliorate concern. I encourage teachers to read them.

I save copies of emails to and notes about my work with each teacher in a folder on my computer and store papers, copies of student work, and other artifacts in a section in my binder. Develop your own system for recording what you do and talk about it with teachers so that you have easy access to your ongoing work together.

First Classroom Observation

A classroom observation is a highly effective way to determine teacher and student strengths and needs. When you schedule your observation, reserve time to reflect on the lesson and plan for your debrief, and schedule a time to debrief, too. If the class is unaccustomed to having visitors, and your presence is unsettling to either the teacher or students, you'll want to observe more than once to get a good feel for them. Prior to your observation, ask the teacher what the students should know about who you are and why you're observing. If students are accustomed to frequent visitors, usually no introductions or explanations are necessary. If classroom visitors are infrequent, a brief introduction may be needed.

When I observe for the first time, the classroom teacher may say something like, "Students, this is Ms. Casey. She and I are going to be working together with you in the next days and weeks. Ms. Casey will be watching us work today to get to know you better and to get to know me better. She's brought her computer and will be taking notes as we work so she doesn't forget anything that happens today. Ms. Casey will be moving around the classroom, listening in to your conversations, maybe visiting table groups or scooting into your partnership conversations or listening in when I confer with you." Letting students know prior to the lesson why I have a laptop, why I like to move around the classroom, and that I really want to get to know them, keeps them from becoming too distracted during the lesson.

Observe Students and Teachers at Work

If the observation follows a conversation with the teacher, use your first observation planning sheet to help shape, but not limit, your observation. If the teacher mentions specific students to observe, prepare name tags for the class in advance so you can identify the students. Decide whether it is more helpful to put name tags on the front or the back of students, or both, depending on your vantage point. Try to notice what the teacher wanted you to focus on, while also noting things that did not come up in conversation. On the one hand, you are trying to observe through the eyes of the teacher to get a feel for the teacher's view of teaching and students. On the other hand, you are observing through your own eyes to offer a second perspective of the classroom dynamics. Coaching is about discussing and negotiating the differences between what the teacher and coach believe are happening in the classroom. It is not about agreeing or seeing things exactly

FIG. 4–7 Observing a student and teacher

the same way or trying to figure out who is right; it is about getting multiple perspectives and gathering data together to inform decision making.

If you haven't had a conversation with the teacher first, you can still use the first observation planning sheet to shape your observation. Analyze student achievement data from the class or grade level. Go through the notes you took during your conversation with the principal to remember what was shared about the teacher. Here's a list of what I usually pay attention to when I observe lessons:

◆ Does the lesson have a clear purpose? Is the purpose leading students to make meaning of text or to communicate meaning in their writing? What is the purpose?

◆ To what degree are students engaged in achieving the purpose?

◆ How is the teacher checking for understanding and making necessary adjustments throughout the lesson?

◆ How are students being led to independence? What do the students know and what can they do as a result of this lesson?

Try to get as close to the students as possible to hear what they are discussing. One of the norms to establish during subsequent visits is how loudly students need to talk so that you can hear their ideas.

Try not to spend your time copying charts; instead, focus on observing and taking notes on what is going on in the classroom. Student-teacher interactions are fleeting—the charts will be there at the end of the lesson.

Take notes on class routines so that when you teach, you are aware of them. What is the teacher's signal for silence? How do students transition from desks to the meeting area and back? How do students get into partnerships or groups? Are students expected to raise their hands? Do students gather in a meeting area for lessons or do they sit at desks? And are the routines as effective and efficient as they can be?

Going into an observation, I try to decide how much I need to capture in my notes, what the teacher wants me to pay attention to, and what I expect will help me discuss possible coaching work. I call it *scripting* when I try to write down what the students or teacher says verbatim so that my notes read back like a transcript of what was said. Alexandra wanted feedback on her questioning strategies, so I scripted as many of her questions as possible. If she wanted feedback on her students' partnership conversations, I would have tried to script her students' conversations. Lessons move quickly, student talk is often hard to hear, and my fingers can only move so fast, so of

Scripting	Note taking
"Where is this story taking place? Do we know the setting? Where? When?"	Asked about setting.
"The writer's opinion is that politicians are corrupt? What led you to that conclusion?"	Asked for evidence and thinking.
"When you're listening to your partner, don't be so quick to agree or disagree. Consider their idea. Linger for a moment and say, 'Hmm . . . what is my partner really saying?'"	Encouraged students to consider ideas.
	Referred to chart to refocus students.
	Called on: Isobel, Moriah, Luke, Antony (×3), Ricardo, Yessica (×2)

FIG. 4–8 Scripting versus note taking

course, my script is incomplete. But even an incomplete script to talk about can help teachers reflect on their own teaching during the debrief. Figure 4–8 is an example of the difference between scripting and note taking.

Both note taking and scripting have value, depending on my purpose. Sometimes I want to tally who speaks, or make a quick schematic of how students are arranged in the lesson, or keep track of how the conversation moves from student to student, or jot down the titles students are reading during independent reading. And sometimes I want to be able to play back the sound of the lesson in my mind and for the teacher.

You may get so captivated with what the students and teacher are discussing that you forget to take notes. Or you may click into teacher mode and want to help the students instead of paying attention to what the teacher is doing. Or you may start mentally planning your debrief conversation. Remember that your responsibility is to *stay in the moment*, carefully observing the students and teacher at work. Jot down stray thoughts and then get back on track with observing and note taking. This is easier said than done—just know that it is important to remain an information-gatherer during your observation and that staying on task requires practice and discipline. Take a look at Figure 4–9 to see how I tried to capture as much as possible on my observation sheet. I took some of the notes during the lesson. The rest I took

Teacher	Alexandra	Grade	7th	Date	10/3

Lesson focus: (*What are students expected to know and be able to do as a result of the lesson?*)

Interactive read-aloud using "Eleven" from *Woman Hollering Creek* by Sandra Cisneros.

To get to know more about characters through their actions, words, and thoughts

Students to focus on:	My notes
Javier—Motivation?	Sliding back from the group, almost underneath the desks on the perimeter of the meeting area.
Mercedes—Motivation?	Initiates talk (x3), responded to partner's thinking.
Miguel—Motivation?	Eye contact with partner as partner shared. Didn't respond or share thinking.
Angelina—Motivation?	Sitting right next to teacher. Hand raised (x4) but out of line of teacher's vision. Stopped raising hand 10 min into lesson.

Classroom environment to focus on:	
Strong community	Quiet class, followed teacher's requests. Do students tend to agree with each other or do they challenge each other's thinking?
	In whole group, 11 girls, 5 boys shared.

Pedagogy to focus on:	
What are students expected to know and be able to do as a result of the lesson?	Students are expected to know how to get to know more about characters through their actions, words, and thoughts.
Supports for English Learners—How is she providing scaffolds for English Learners?	?? Not sure yet.
Questioning strategies	(see page of scripted questions)
Use of think-aloud	"I'm thinking that by slowing us down and really describing how Rachel pushed the sweater to the edge of her desk, Sandra Cisneros is helping us imagine and experience Rachel's embarrassment and disgust." *Continues*

FIG. 4–9 Filled out observation sheet

Classroom Routines:

Signal for silence	Transitions	Seating arrangements (student-selected, seating plan?)
"All eyes on me." Raises hand, when students notice they raise their hands and stop talking. Works really well.	"Table 1, join us in the meeting area." 8 tables Sends students off to work when ready.	Students select partners in meeting area. Each beginning ELL joins a pair so they can hear the conversations (and participate when able). Desks are assigned, pretty much by who works well with whom.
How do students keep track of their learning? (notebooks, take notes?) Students have reading notebooks and a separate notebook for word study. Brought notebooks to meeting area but didn't use them during lesson.	**How do students get to share thinking and work?** (bring a few kids up, share in partnerships, called on one at a time?) Students partner talked throughout lesson. Some called on to share thinking in whole group. Others volunteered.	**How do students formalize or generalize their learning for the day?** (in writing, with partners, as a class?) Not sure. Charts around the room show examples of how to write about thinking, and various responses to texts.

Other notes:

Classroom library has easily accessible baskets of books (mostly all fiction).

How does work get selected for display on the bulletin boards?

Cool way to display the texts students recommend!

Can all students see the overhead when they're in the meeting area?

FIG. 4–9 Cont.

as I reflected on the lesson in the hall, just after I left Alexandra's room. I try to leave five to ten minutes between observations so that I have time to jot down my thoughts before heading into another teacher's classroom. Figure 4–10 is a blank observation sheet for your use or you may want to create your own.

Teacher _____	Grade _____ Date _____

Lesson focus: *(What are students expected to know and be able to do as a result of the lesson?)*

Students to focus on: **Notes:**

Classroom environment to focus on:

Pedagogy to focus on:

Continues

FIG. 4–10 Observation planning sheet

Classroom Routines:		
Signal for silence	**Transitions**	**Seating arrangements** (student-selected, seating plan?)
How do students keep track of their learning? (notebooks, take notes?)	**How do students get to share thinking and work?** (bring a few kids up, share in partner-ships, called on one at a time?)	**How do students for-malize or generalize their learning for the** day? (in writing, with partners, as a class?)

Other notes:

_____

_____

_____

FIG. 4–10 Cont.

Some coaches write a quick thank-you note with a debrief meeting reminder and leave it with the teacher on the way out of the classroom.

Alexandra,

Thank you so much for welcoming me into your classroom so that I could get to know you and your students better. I'm looking forward to our debrief meeting at 2:15 this afternoon in your room.

Have a great rest of the day,

Katherine

What May My Coaching Work with This Teacher Involve?

With your first classroom observation(s) complete, you now have quite a bit of information to process. Most teachers are really curious about what you thought of their students and lesson and will want to talk with you as soon as possible. Try to schedule your debrief for the same day or next day. Your immediate concern may be what to talk about in your debrief. Before jumping into planning for your debrief, take some time to analyze the information you've gathered, craft a preliminary plan for your coaching work, and choose a leverage point. You want to have short- and long-term ideas in mind—knowing that your work with another teacher is a relationship, and as such, should evolve as you communicate more together—before you have a debrief.

Brainstorm Long-Term and Short-Term Goals; Choose a Leverage Point

One of the challenges you may face when beginning to develop a plan for your coaching relationship with a teacher is that you are not sure where to start. Keep in mind that this is an ongoing relationship with the teacher and that you'll have multiple opportunities to work together. The only way to help teachers become better decision makers and reflective practition ers is to do so over time. If your schedule allows only a few opportunities to work with a teacher, know that the effect your work will have on teaching and learning may be minimal. Change is a process of continual revision over time, with highs and lows, frustration and elation, successes and missteps.

Spread out all the information you've gathered so far—from your analysis of student data and discussion with the teacher about student strengths and needs; from your conversation with the teacher about her strengths, needs, and what she needs for her learning; and from the classroom observation—and begin to craft a plan for your work. At this point you are developing a theory (an idea or belief about something arrived at through speculation or conjecture) based on the information you have. Your theory will shift and change as you collaborate with the teacher over time.

Start with Strengths

Begin to create a theory about which areas of strength can be built on and figure out how you might use those strengths over time in your work. Some possibilities:

- ◆ What is the teacher already doing that is enabling students to be successful?
  - igniting students' excitement for learning?
  - teaching for meaning?
  - planning based on student needs?
  - assessing students and adjusting during the lesson?
  - using evidence of student understanding to plan next lessons?
  - clear and appropriate focus?
  - choosing the appropriate level of support?
  - pacing?
  - modeling?
  - visual supports?
  - text selection?
  - connecting lessons to prior lessons and future work?
  - consideration of grade-level standards and expectations?
- ◆ What is the teacher already doing that with slight adjustment could be even more supportive for students?
- ◆ Does the teacher do something strong during writing lessons that could be utilized in reading lessons or vice versa?
- ◆ What has the teacher expressed a desire to know and be able to do that can be a focus of the work?
- ◆ What are the students already doing well?

Alexandra's classroom community was collaborative and students eagerly shared their ideas with each other. What a strength! However, student talk lingered at the literal level, perhaps because students wanted to encourage each other and thought challenging each other or veering from the literal would rock the boat. I brainstormed possible ways Alexandra and I could teach the students how to collaborate in becoming critical thinkers about texts and life. Looking around her room, it is clear Alexandra took care to prepare charts to focus the lesson and created co-constructed charts during the lesson. But the charts tended to be text specific. With some support, I anticipated that Alexandra could think about and use charting to help students move toward independence. Also, because Alexandra expressed a desire to improve her questioning strategies, I planned to use questioning as a lens to help us focus on pushing student talk and reconstructing her charts.

Shift to Areas of Need

After examining both the students' and teacher's strengths, start listing areas of need. Remember, you're creating a tentative theory that will change and shift over time. Your list may be long and may contain ideas that are inaccurate. After all, it is based on conversations with the teacher and limited classroom observations! Nevertheless, brainstorming the most detailed list possible is helpful because you can sort, classify, and prioritize the ideas into possible long-term and short-term goals for your coaching work. Also, not everything on the list of needs will be addressed directly in classroom coaching. Instead, some topics may be addressed in whole-school, grade/department-level, or small-group staff development, especially if you notice a pattern across classrooms.

Here's what I brainstormed, in the order in which the ideas came to me, for my work with Alexandra. You can use the list to help think about your own teachers' practice.

◆ Teach for meaning making—how to help students learn to make meaning of texts.
◆ Shift pacing from time retelling text to critically thinking about ideas in text.
◆ Look at seating arrangement—off-task students are hiding in teacher's blind spots.
◆ Think about how to use standards for instructional planning without making them the focus of the lesson.
◆ Shift questioning away from literal to critical; shift away from stacking questions.
◆ Try to chunk text—decide how much to read at a time before students talk about text.
◆ Model—what to model and when to think aloud.
◆ Model charting for independence—how to create charts that students can refer to when reading and writing independently.
◆ Introduce English Learner supports—show how to support their movement beyond the literal.

Choose a Leverage Point

Once you've assessed strengths and areas of need, you'll see lots of possible ways to direct your coaching work. Addressing each area one by one is neither feasible nor practical, since the decision-making process required of teachers is multifaceted and interwoven. So how do you figure out what to focus on? Work to determine a leverage point. A leverage point can be understood as the point in a process where an intervention can have the greatest effect (Knight 2001). When a leverage point is addressed, a number of subsequent steps in the process will be addressed as well. To have the greatest effect, the leverage point needs to be within the teacher's zone of proximal development (ZPD) (Vygotsky 1962) and needs to be within your capability as a coach.

Lucy Calkins says, "conferring with young readers (as with young writers) first involves *research* in order to learn where the child is as a reader and understand the child's intention, then *deciding* what we should teach, and then *teaching* in a way that can influence what that child does on another day with another book" (Calkins 2000). Similarly, when choosing a leverage point, I think about the research I've gathered that helps me get a feel for where teacher is and understand the teacher's intention, and I decide what I should teach the teacher. Then I teach in a way that can influence what the teacher does on another day with another lesson.

Asking yourself questions will help you determine your leverage point. Figure 4–11 shows how I tried to figure out the right leverage point for Alexandra.

After considering possible underlying causes of Alexandra's areas of need and their connection to each other, I brainstormed a rough action plan of how I might address each over time, based on the following conclusions:

◆ The principal's goal in professional development is for teachers to increase the rigor in what they are teaching students to know and be able to do. For the English department, the focus is on reading, since standards test results in reading are lower than in writing.

◆ Alexandra is working on questioning strategies with her department.

◆ Alexandra doesn't consider read-aloud her strength because she's not confident the students are engaged with her.

◆ I'll need to be able to demonstrate anything I suggest because Alexandra wants demonstration, preferably as she teaches.

Brainstormed list of needs	My thinking about the question, "Is this the leverage point?"
Teaching for meaning making	That's going to be the focus of everything we do. Plan to read and discuss a variety of texts together, have conversations about why we read and what we want students to know and be able to do as readers, and so on. In theory, this is a terrific leverage point because by focusing on what we want to teach, we can better consider how we want to teach them. But in reality, it is probably outside of Alexandra's zone of proximal development (ZPD) because the idea is so big.
Shift away from literal to critical thinking	Why does Alexandra linger on the literal? Does she know she does? Does she have planning and teaching strategies to use to go beyond the literal toward meaning making? What's her understanding of the big ideas in the text? Another ongoing focus for our work together.
Seating arrangement	Not a leverage point for Alexandra. She is demonstrating a solid understanding of the power of seating arrangements already. After all, she is a middle school teacher who gets thirty-eight students to sit in a circle for text discussions! Changing seats won't have a big ripple effect. Just let her know students in her blind spots are off task. Problem-solve seating arrangements. In a demo, model how to move students around and how to explain to students why they're being moved (and help teach them take responsibility for staying on task).
Role of standards in instructional planning	Ties back to the idea that purpose of reading is to make meaning, not to "do" the standards. What's Alexandra's understanding of the role of standards? How does she use them in instructional planning? Start talking about this with her. Plan to demonstrate meaning-making lesson that embeds standards-based work.
Questioning	Alexandra wants help in this area and has support from her department. Certainly within her ZPD. Could open the door to conversations about meaning making, critical thinking, English Learner supports, chunking texts, standards, etc.
Chunking texts	Why is she stopping so often? How does she make decisions about when to stop? What is her understanding of chunking as a support for helping students make meaning? Chunking may be a good leverage point because it could be a way into conversations about meaning, teaching for transference, questioning, modeling, etc.
	Continues

FIG. 4–11 Determining a leverage point

Modeling	Seems big and ongoing, and connected to how to teach students to make meaning. Alexandra says she wants support in this area. Goes back to instructional planning, too—what does Alexandra want students to know and be able to do as a result of the lesson? Goes back to role of the standards—Does Alexandra think the purpose is to perform standard for the sake of performing the standard? Another big topic to address long term in a variety of ways (especially by modeling for Alexandra).
Charting for independence	Too concrete for a leverage point for Alexandra, but could be another window into thinking about the purpose and student outcomes of a lesson. What we chart and why is a result of what we know about lesson design and teaching for transference to independence. Perhaps charting can be addressed by looking at questioning and/or lesson planning?
English Learner supports	Another big and ongoing topic. How to differentiate instruction for a group of students will follow how to plan instruction for a large group of students. Begin to embed English Learner supports when modeling for and working alongside Alexandra.

FIG. 4–11 Cont.

◆ I need to build on strengths, and Alexandra wants support in questioning. She's planning her questions according to her understanding of how to help students reach standards.

◆ During her lesson I felt like she was chunking the text too much. Maybe because she wants to think aloud and ask enough questions?

◆ My leverage point needs to be within her ZPD and needs to have a ripple effect on other aspects of her teaching.

From my developing theory, I decided that focusing on Alexandra's questioning might be a good starting leverage point. I reviewed the notes I took during Alexandra's lesson to remind me of the only picture I had so far of her decision making as she taught. I isolated her questions to the class to see if I had evidence that questioning is a good place to start (see Figure 4–12). What do you notice about Alexandra's questioning strategies?

Notice that Alexandra tends to stack her questions, meaning she tends to ask three or four questions right in a row before giving students a chance to speak.

Alexandra's questions (from my notes on her lesson)	My thinking that I jotted after her lesson
Text: "Eleven" by Sandra Cisneros Approach: interactive read-aloud Purpose: To get to know more about characters through their actions, words, and thoughts. What is she saying right here? Do you guys understand that? I'll read it again. Picture it in your mind. Look. I'll show you with these wooden dolls. What does she mean? How does the narrator feel, telling you the story? What does that tell us about the teacher? Is she maybe scared or embarrassed? Now I want you to talk to your partner, what are you learning about Rachel from thoughts, actions? What are we learning about this person? If you can give me an answer give me evidence, too. What is this telling you about how this person is feeling? Do we know how she feels about her teacher? How do we know? When you get older and wiser, you know what to say. Is that how she feels? [Alexandra kept reading] What is happening to Rachel? What are her actions telling us? What would be a good inference? What would be a good idea? Would you feel that way? Can you see that? Do you notice how she's moving that chair? The sweater is to the right, just hanging there. Do you see how she's quietly trying to defy the teacher? How is the teacher acting right now?	Seems to stack her questions, meaning she asks a few right in a row before giving students time to answer. The stacked questions are slightly different. Could that be confusing to the students? Are the questions leading students to a line of thinking? Seeking evidence in the text—do students think they just have to quote text? If so, reinforces literal thinking.

FIG. 4–12 Alexandra's questions

The stacked questions have slightly different meanings—for example, "What is happening to Rachel? What are her actions telling us? What would be a good inference? What would be a good idea?"—which may lead students to be unsure of what they should be talking about. Some of Alexandra's questions are also leading students to follow her line of thinking rather than develop their own line of thinking. Also, when Alexandra pushes students for evidence in the text, she tends to accept quotes or retelling without probing for thinking work using a prompt such as, "Yes, that's what the text says" and not, "What are you thinking about what the text says?" I also remembered that Alexandra told me she had prewritten questions in the margin of the text to ask. Were the questions in the margins the ones she asked or was she creating her questions in the moment?

Questioning strategies connected to how to chunk the text and how to help students learn to make meaning of texts became my beginning leverage point for work with Alexandra. Could I have chosen another leverage point? Possibly, but I based my decision on my best thinking given the information I had gathered, even though I expected everything to shift and change in response to our ongoing coaching relationship. I hoped that by beginning to help Alexandra become aware of how she currently uses questioning strategies, I could open the door to working with her on our ultimate goal: teaching students to construct meaning as they read independently.

Choosing a leverage point continues to be a challenge for me, and often what we start working on together shifts quickly in response to the teacher's and students' evolving needs and my evolving understanding of the teacher's practice. When I first started coaching, I wasn't really sure how to even observe and analyze lessons, let alone choose a leverage point that might help shift a teacher's practice. As you coach more, you'll develop a sense of what teachers may need next for their practice. You'll try things that work and others that don't get you as far as you hoped, and then you'll try something else.

 ## Prepare for the First Observation Debrief

Once you have determined a leverage point, it is time to start preparing for your debrief conversation. A debrief meeting is different from a post-conference typically done after an evaluation, in which the evaluator may ask the teacher to reflect on the lesson, may make evaluative statements, and then may provide suggested next steps. Unlike the evaluator who evaluates and gives feedback to a teacher once or a few times a year—feedback that may be devoid of any reference to the supports necessary to help the teacher implement suggested changes—you are involved in an ongoing relationship of support and growth. It will be up to you to demonstrate any suggestions you make to the teacher. You will be responsible for working with the teacher to problem-solve and make the changes necessary to accelerate students' learning.

Your teacher may expect your debrief meeting to run like an evaluation post-conference and may bring any positive or negative feelings she has about the post-conference process with her. Teachers accustomed to nothing but praise may bristle at any suggestions for growth. Anticipate that you'll need to explain that a debrief meeting is really a continuation of your initial conversation with the teacher—when you discussed student and teacher strengths and areas of need—and one that will evolve and deepen throughout your work together.

The purpose of the debrief meeting is to share observations about the students and teacher, to discuss next steps, and to formulate a plan for upcoming work together. Gather your thoughts before you meet. What you'll talk about during the first debrief depends on what your coaching plan with the teacher entails. Are you going to work together tomorrow? If so, focus on what you learned today that may help you plan tomorrow's work. Or do you have a few days until you work together again? Whatever the schedule, starting with the notes written on your first observation planning sheet is a good idea, especially if you gave a copy of it to the teacher before your observation.

Keep the students in the center of the conversation. Doing so will take the edge off the teacher, who may feel that you are judging her. Rather than asking, "How do you feel the lesson went?" try asking, "What did you learn about your students in the lesson?" Share what you observed particular students saying and doing. Compliment strong aspects of the teacher's practice. Take an inquiry stance and ask about how and why the teacher made decisions during the lesson. Ask the teacher what he wants to know from you about the lesson. Don't forget that this is the beginning on an ongoing relationship and that, as such, both of you may feel hesitant and awkward until you establish your conversational style. Decide on the next steps for your upcoming work together.

Use the notes you took during your observation to discuss the leverage point. By taking copious notes during the lesson, you can better review what happened in the lesson together. I often start by having the teacher read through what I wrote, saying, "I took notes on as much of your lesson as I could so that we can use what happened in the lesson in our conversation. Though I know my notes couldn't capture everything that happened in the lesson, I think it will give us a good starting place. Would you like to read through them to get the sound of the lesson back in your mind?" Usually teachers start to make reflective comments about their teaching: "I see that the same student is answering my questions. How many children contributed? Did I really spend eight minutes on the intro? It felt much faster to me. I ask a lot of questions. Did you understand what that child was trying to say? I didn't know those two students spoke so much in partner talk." Having detailed notes allows the teacher to relive and reflect on her practice, prompting her to make observations about her students and teaching. The more we can help teachers self-discover aspects of their teaching, the better.

Once you've raised the teacher's awareness about possible growth areas, you are ready to start thinking and talking about how you might support the teacher during your next coaching session. Have suggestions ready, such as the professional development structures described in Part II, and be open to negotiating your role.

An Ongoing Process of Getting Started

Just as getting to know students' strengths and needs isn't a one-time event, getting to know a teacher's strengths and areas of need is not a one-time activity. You will engage in a process of analyzing your teachers' instructional practice, their students' performance, their participation in professional development opportunities, and the types of supports that make a difference in their practice. When I am unsure of how to support a teacher, I am reminded of when I first started conferring with readers and writers, not sure what to ask or listen for, not sure if the decisions I made were the right ones. Once I stopped worrying about figuring out the right response and focused on listening to what children were telling and showing me, let go of trying to "fix" their work, and asked children what support they needed from me, I heard their intentions, started to view their writing and reading process through their eyes, and with the children's help, found my teaching points. Encourage your teachers to help you hear their intentions, view their teaching through their eyes and through their students' eyes, and find your teaching points. The chapters in Part II describe a variety of ways to organize professional development to support your teachers' growth.

Part II   Structures for Professional Development

Because literacy coaches provide learning experiences for a diverse group of educators, we require a variety of professional development structures that offer many kinds of support. Many times it makes sense to work on professional development in classrooms with real-life students and teachers. At other times, it makes sense to gather together away from children and even away from our school building to engage in professional study and inquiry, network with fellow educators, read and discuss professional texts, study student work and create lessons, or analyze our instruction on videotape. In any of these settings, group size may vary from the whole staff to small groups to individual teachers, depending on the participants' needs.

These several professional development structures are divided among the next three chapters. In Chapter 5, we start with structures that help address the question, "What does instruction look and sound like?" These include:

- Demonstrating lessons
- Intravisitations and intervisitations
- Purposeful involvement while observing lessons
- Lesson study
- Co-planning lessons

If building a common vision of instruction were as simple as showing teachers a lesson or two, then a few demonstrations would be enough. But since we know that the work of creating and teaching effective lessons is far more complex, professional development structures are organized along a continuum that begins with observing, analyzing, and evaluating existing lessons; moves to cocreating and evaluating new lessons; and gradually releases to co-planning lessons. Then we shift to structures that allow us to gather together for professional study away from the bustle of our classrooms:

- Attending professional development conferences
- Joining in professional inquiry groups
- Videotaping and analyzing lessons

In Chapter 6 we turn our attention to intense, classroom-based professional development structures. Both the gradual release and the unit of study coaching cycles create ongoing opportunities for you to work side-by-side in the same classroom over time, providing teachers and students with highly supportive coaching.

Chapter 7 focuses on the guiding principles of designing adult learning in meetings, workshops, and inservice programs, and shows how to design and facilitate such professional development sessions.

In Chapter 8 we are encouraged to keep in mind that when we craft effective professional development experiences, literacy coaching has the power to transform teaching and learning.

As you read these next chapters, keep in mind what you know about individual teachers, groups of teachers, and your whole staff. Think about the culture of your school; about already-established opportunities for learning that could be modified to include some of these structures; and about the reality of your and your teachers' schedules.

Which structures you use will depend on *what* you want teachers to know and be able to do; on *which* teachers will be engaged in the learning; and on *how* the teachers learn best. The supports we provide for teachers should take into account the National Staff Development Council's "Standards for Staff Development" (2001), as well as address the essential features of effective professional development (Darling-Hammond and McLaughlin 1995):

- It must be grounded in inquiry, reflection, and experimentation that are participant driven.

◆ It must be collaborative and involve the sharing of knowledge among educators and a focus on communities of practice rather than on individual teachers.

◆ It must be sustained, ongoing, intensive, and supported by modeling, coaching, and the collective solving of specific problems of practice.

◆ It must be connected to and derived from teachers' work with their students.

◆ It must engage teachers in concrete tasks of teaching, assessment, observation, and reflection that illuminate the processes of learning and development.

Eight Ways to Study Instruction

You just spent time thinking about how to determine your teachers' strengths and needs so that you can figure out what they need for their learning. By now you've read the phrase "provide your teachers with the supports they need for their learning" so many times that you know what's coming next: supports. You're right. Sounds simple enough. You figure out what your teachers' strengths and needs are and then you address their needs. But how, exactly, do you do that? I can't tell you specifically how to address each teacher's needs because coaching is an art, not a science. What I can do is offer you eight ways to study instruction with your teachers. Not all of these may be appropriate for your learners or your school culture (yet) or within your skill set as a coach (yet). If you find yourself saying, "sounds good, but I'm not sure how to do some of these things," start with the ones that feel comfortable so that your early experiences with teachers are successful. And make time to gain experience with the ones that are unfamiliar so that you broaden your coaching repertoire. This is a good time to remember, also, how important it is to cast yourself as a learner and not an expert, so that teachers bear with you as you try on new professional development structures.

In the upcoming sections, I try to help you visualize each kind of activity; include the rationale and my guiding questions for each to help make my decision making transparent; and, when appropriate, offer examples of how other literacy coaches use these ways with their teachers. The question is, as always, what makes sense for your work?

Demonstrating Lessons

Showing people what instruction looks like and sounds like is vital to successful coaching. By teaching students with other teachers watching, you gain credibility as an educator; in order to believe in you as a coach, teachers need to see you as a capable teacher. You begin to gain the trust of your teachers as you model risk taking and a willingness to grow professionally. You bring pedagogical strategies to life for people to view, experience, analyze, and apply to their own teaching. And let's be honest, if you can't walk the walk as well as talk the talk, then you cannot provide teachers with what so many say they need for their learning—to see teaching and learning work with their students. That said, no one is a perfect teacher and there is no such thing as a perfect lesson, which is why I hesitate to use the term *demonstration lesson*, and prefer, instead, to say that I am demonstrating a lesson. You should clearly and repeatedly communicate to teachers that whenever you demonstrate a lesson, you are doing the best work you know how to do at that moment, with ample room for revision and improvement to better meet students' needs.

What you choose to demonstrate, with whom, and why should be based on the needs of the teachers for whom you are demonstrating. Note the use of the plural—teachers. Whenever possible, try not to demonstrate a lesson for one teacher because when you leave the room, the teacher has no one with whom to discuss the lesson. You want to build capacity and opportunities to collaborate within a group of teachers, so if you're planning to demonstrate a lesson, try to schedule a time when a few teachers can observe or when substitute teachers are available.

Much goes into the success of a demonstration lesson. The Demonstration Lesson Planning Page in Figure 5–1 can help you organize your planning work. When I demonstrate a lesson, I consider numerous factors.

Teacher Learning Outcomes: What Do I Want the Teachers to Know and Be Able to Do as a Result of Demonstrating a Lesson?

Start with a clear purpose for why you are demonstrating a lesson. What are you trying to demonstrate? What do you want teachers to see you do? To see the students do? The clearer you can be about what effect you expect demonstrating a lesson will have on the teachers, the more purposeful demonstrating a lesson can be.

☐ Lesson Plan   Date_____

☐ Copy of Text / Materials

☐ Look for Sheet

☐ Student Name Tags

Planning for teachers:

What will the teachers know and be able to do as a result of my coaching (long-term)?

What will I model in this lesson based on my coaching focus?

What will support the teachers in observing the lesson?

Planning for students:

What do I want students to know and be able to do as a result of the lesson?

How do I plan to get them there?

© 2006 by Katherine Casey from *Literacy Coaching*. Portsmouth, NH: Heinemann.

FIG. 5–1 Demonstration Lesson Planning Page

The following is a short list of different purposes I had for recent lessons I demonstrated:

◆ Teachers want to see how I scaffold students in making meaning of a short informational text from a set of recently purchased curriculum materials. I want teachers to observe and name the scaffolds I use as a beginning to a professional study of how to teach students to read informational texts. I want to arouse teachers' curiosity about the curriculum materials so that they start using them with their students.

◆ Teachers are grappling with how to help their students become more critical of the materials they read on the Internet. During the lesson, I'll demonstrate for teachers how I use a split overhead (two texts on the same transparency about the same topic from two different Internet sites) to begin a conversation with students about being critical readers of Internet materials.

◆ Kindergarten teachers have students reading by themselves during independent reading. We've read and discussed professional texts that explain the power of partner reading, but the management seems overwhelming. Teachers want to see how I model partner reading for the students.

◆ Teachers report that their students complain about having to reread texts. I want to demonstrate how I present rereading to students (shifting the students' attitude from, "If you don't understand it the first time, reread" to, "In order to actually understand a text, we need to read it more than once").

◆ The district is introducing shared writing as an instructional approach for beginning English Language Learners. In a series of lessons (three short lessons in an hour) for the upper-grade teachers with beginning English Language Learners, I plan to demonstrate English language development strategies. We'll use what we learned from observing and analyzing the lessons to frame our lesson-planning work.

◆ High school teachers want to see what teaching reading in the content areas looks like. Using tenth-grade students who, the teachers report, are "years behind" in their learning, I plan to model strategies we read about in our professional text study.

Student Selection

The students you decide to teach when you demonstrate a lesson should be chosen purposefully, because the selection can make or break the success of your demonstration. If teachers feel the students reflect their students, they can see the application to their teaching more clearly. When you are demonstrating a lesson at the request of a grade level of teachers, encourage them to select the class, so they have ownership in the demonstration process. When your lesson is part of ongoing work in a coaching cycle with a group of teachers, you may decide, depending on your purpose, to rotate your demonstrations from class to class over time, or to demonstrate a number of lessons in the same classroom to show how teaching and learning shift over time.

When you demonstrate a lesson during a whole-staff conference, it is harder to select the right group of students. Try to choose students who represent the majority of students in your school. If you have a high concentration of English Language Learners, select a classroom with a high concentration of English Language Learners. If you have many students who can word-call beautifully but lack comprehension skills, select a class of word callers who need comprehension strategies. When I demonstrate lessons at whole-staff conferences, I share some of the data on the class as a whole and ask teachers to consider the students in their classes who seem similar, to jot down their students' names, and to keep them in mind as I teach so that they can consider the applicability of the pedagogical strategies to their work with their students.

Early in your coaching work, be extremely cautious about demonstrating lessons with a group of students the staff considers easy to teach—unless the majority of the staff or your principal makes the request. During my first year of teaching I participated in a unit-of-study coaching cycle in a classroom comprised of students in a gifted and talented program. I just couldn't concentrate on the lessons because I spent the entire time thinking, "This would *never* work with my students." Later I learned that the instructional strategies worked with all students and that there are no easy classes because all students present their teachers with challenges, but at the time I just couldn't get past how different the coach's class seemed from mine. Not until she started demonstrating lessons with groups of students whose needs were similar to my students' was I able to actually pay attention to the pedagogical strategies she was demonstrating. Now I can observe lessons with any group of students, regardless of age and perceived ability, and pay attention to the effective teaching moves. But my observational skills took years to build. Many teachers with whom I work concur. Context matters. We need to see things work with our students, or students who are similar to ours.

Teachers as Students

Sometimes I have the teachers participate in a lesson as their students so they can develop a sense of what a lesson looks and feels like. We often teach as we were taught, especially when we tread into unfamiliar curricular areas, because it is so challenging to teach in a way we haven't been taught. The more teachers can experience as learners the type of instruction they will use with their students, the better. I have attended multiple summer workshops on teaching reading, writing, and mathematics in which the leaders engaged us in learning that replicated, effective teaching practices. To teach us how to teach writing, instructors led us through the writing process as writers; to teach us how to teach reading, instructors led us through the reading process as readers; and to teach us to teach mathematics, instructors led us through mathematical experiences as mathematicians. Putting teachers in the role of students helps them know what it feels like to be a learner.

If you decide to have the teachers participate as your students in a lesson, provide them with the rationale for your decision. I usually say, "Today I'm going to teach one lesson in a series of lessons designed to teach students to make meaning of complex informational texts. Rather than do the lesson with a group of students, I'm going to have you be the students, for a number of reasons. First, some of us have said that we just don't know what it feels like to be a student during a shared reading lesson. This experience may help. Second, some of us questioned why a teacher models throughout a shared reading lesson. You'll get to experience if and how the modeling helps your meaning making. Third, you know that I believe we cannot teach what we don't know, and if we don't experience the power of an instructional approach, how can we use that approach effectively?"

When you are working with a large group of teachers, you may want to fishbowl the lesson by having some of the teachers engage in the lesson as the students while the other teachers observe them. As always, base your decisions on thoughtful consideration of your adult learners.

Student Learning Outcomes: What Do I Want the Students to Know and Be Able to Do as a Result of the Lesson I'm Demonstrating?

Planning for what students should know and be able to do as a result of the lesson you demonstrate is also critical and should, ideally, involve discussion with their classroom teacher. If you are demonstrating a lesson as part of ongoing coaching work in a teacher's classroom, you have a sense of what the students need next for their learning. But getting to know the students firsthand is not always possible, and you'll need to rely on phone calls or emails to gather information.

When I work as a consultant, I rarely have an opportunity to spend time in a teacher's classroom before beginning our work, which makes planning a lesson based on knowledge of student and teacher strengths and areas of need especially difficult. In these cases I rely on emails to build or strengthen a relationship with the teacher and students.

Last year I worked periodically with a group of elementary and secondary teachers in Nooksack Valley School District in Washington State. My visits were one part of ongoing professional development opportunities that brought educators together to work on improving their practice. A few weeks before each visit, Assistant Superintendent Sandy Austin emailed me indicating what teachers had decided they and their students needed next for their learning. Sandy's email prompted a flurry of email correspondence as we narrowed our focus and crafted agendas for my four-day visit. Lessons were frequently requested, requiring me to gather as much information as possible about the students from the teachers hosting my lessons. Figure 5–2 shows my correspondence with one fourth-grade teacher, Lisa Shafer. The next day I received a response from Lisa (see Figure 5–3), filled with valuable information.

Sometimes, you won't be able to find out much, if anything, about the students before you work with them. When that happens, refer to the grade-level standards for ideas about what students should be working on in that grade level.

When your students are adults, it is still necessary to design a lesson with clear learning outcomes. Create a lesson plan just as you would if you were teaching children, and be prepared to discuss how you designed your lesson. When I teach a lesson to adults, I often say something like, "When I planned this lesson I had our fourth graders in mind. The text I selected and the meaning-making work I'm emphasizing is with their needs in mind." Make your planning process visible by providing teachers with a copy of your lesson plan.

Using Materials Teachers Have or Can Immediately Access

When you design a lesson, be considerate of the materials you use with the students. If teachers are limited in what they can use for instructional

> Hi Lisa,
>
> I hope your year with your fourth graders started out well. I am looking forward to having a chance to work with you and your students on Monday, October 25. Thank you in advance for letting me work with your students.
>
> Sandy, Anneke, and I discussed the focus for the work that day based on the district's fourth- and fifth-grade teachers' feedback. We'll be working on reading lessons, of course (either shared or read aloud, depending on the level of support your students need for their learning), conferring during independent reading, and student engagement.
>
> Here's what would help make my work stronger. Would you please let me know what your students have been working on as readers so far this year? Are you focusing on particular reading strategies? Or genres? Are there authors or titles students have really enjoyed?
>
> What types of texts are students reading during independent reading?
>
> If you have a moment to spare, please just jot down a brief response so that I can get a sense of what's going on with your students these days. If you have anything you want me to explicitly model, let me know.
>
> If you have any questions for me, please let me know.
>
> With appreciation,
>
> Katherine

FIG. 5–2 Email to Lisa

materials—for example, everything has to come from the textbook series—then use textbook series materials unless you and your principal are willing and able to revise policy. If teachers are encouraged to supplement their textbooks with additional materials, then demonstration lessons can be an effective way to show teachers the possibilities that exist outside their textbook. When teachers have full control of what they can select to use with students, your text selection can be broad.

Hi Katherine—We are basking in the sunshine up here *but* as you know, it won't last for long. It is going to be sunny all week and rainy the next. I sure hope you see a little bit of everything while you're here and not just the rain.

OK—down to business about the 25th. I have twenty-one fourth graders and here is a little background that might be helpful/interesting. I have four Native American students, six Hispanic students, and eleven Caucasian students. It is a pretty mellow class with the only real issue being chattiness.

As readers we have been focusing on "turn and talk" in response to a question during read-alouds. We have done some small-group discussions. I have been working on asking questions (like you taught us . . .) that try to get them beyond retell. For example, the read-aloud we just finished was *Carlotta's Kittens* by Phyllis Reynolds Naylor. The kids did some talking and then writing work around the following question: What did the kittens learn about life in the human world? I am hoping my questions aren't too broad yet give some room for all levels to participate actively. They really enjoyed this book and seem to relate to the feelings of growing up, leaving mom someday, learning how to care for yourself, etc.

Our next read-aloud is historical fiction from the Dear America series. It is titled *Across the Wide and Lonesome Prairie: The Oregon Trail Diary of Hattie Campbell*. The two fourth grades are in the midst of a social studies unit on the Oregon Trail. We are doing most of our reading and writing around this topic. The kids are used to writing reading responses in their reading logs. They also have separate writing journals/diaries if that helps. We use draft books for writing work that requires more time to plan and draft:

During independent reading time they are each reading a book: book clubs are reading Pony Pals: *Give Me Back My Pony, Pony for Keeps, The Littles to the Rescue,* or *The Original Littles.* These kids all have a buddy in the same book. We also have six kids reading a Rigby level 18–20 fiction or nonfiction. I have seven kids reading Dan Gutman's *The Kid who Ran for President.* Book browsing is allowed, although we don't have tons of time for it. My sharp readers (use time wisely) are also all reading some type of fiction on their own.

FIG. 5–3 Lisa's email

Strategies—We have mainly been focusing on their role as active readers. They are working hard to reread when meaning breaks down, to check at the end of each page (Do I understand what I just read or was I thinking about spaghetti for dinner?) and to ask themselves questions about the basic literary elements of plot, character, and setting. With our new read-aloud we are learning about the features of historical fiction. They have also learned the features of nonfiction text.

Well—I am not sure if this is what you need. Please don't worry about asking for more clarification . . . although, I may not know the answer!! We are up and running in fourth grade . . . I think you will enjoy this group of kids.

FIG. 5–3 Cont.

If your students are teachers, select materials that are engaging for adults. This does not mean that you have to select adult-level materials. In fact, some of the most effective lessons I demonstrate occur when I show people how to use student materials more effectively. For example, after I modeled how to help students talk about the big ideas in Amy Hest's *You Can Do It, Sam*, all my kindergarten teachers used it with their students and reported being surprised by how a seemingly simple text could spark such lively conversation about big ideas like gaining confidence and the power of love.

Make copies for the teachers of any materials you use with the students. If you use excerpts from longer texts, put the full reference on the copy so teachers know the source of the materials. Because I'm continually trying to broaden teachers' knowledge of terrific texts, I also bring along similar materials so I can say, "If you liked this text, you might like these."

Repeated Lessons

Anything worth learning is going to take time to learn. Repetition is one of the necessary conditions of learning. Here are some hints for teaching repeated lessons:

- ◆ Because learning happens gradually, teachers always ask, "What would you do tomorrow with the students?" In order to show "tomorrow," plan to teach a series of lessons with the same class. Scheduling may be an obstacle, especially if you have only one day in a particular school.

Consider teaching two lessons with the same class on the same day. For example, if you have ninety minutes for a professional development session, you might teach the students for twenty minutes, have them leave while you process the lesson with the teachers, and bring the students back for another twenty-minute lesson. That way you can show teachers two consecutive lessons and you have the advantage of working with a group of students you know a little in the second lesson.

◆ The act of teaching involves decision making. As we work to understand pedagogy and content, we ask questions like, "Do you always . . . ?" or "Do you ever . . . ?" or "What would you do if . . . ?" In order to show teachers how you make decisions based on student needs, show them a variety of situations with a variety of students.

◆ Model a variety of strategies and lessons. Teachers try on what they see is effective for students. If we model only a few effective teaching techniques, or only certain types of lessons, teachers may inadvertently overutilize the techniques. In one district I taught two reading lessons using narrative texts and had students "turn and talk" to their partners throughout the lessons. A month later I returned to the district, taught an expository text reading lesson and this time had students "turn and talk" as well as "stop and jot" their thinking. As I taught, I heard a murmur from the observing teachers, who shared with me after the lesson that they didn't know they could have students stop and jot and they didn't know that they could use expository texts because my previous lessons only involved turning and talking about narrative texts.

We need to experience things repeatedly in order to make meaning. Parents can attest to the hundreds of times they show, explain, and tell their children the same thing before the child internalizes the learning. And brain research reveals that in order for us to consolidate understanding, we need repetition and reinforcement over time in our preferred modality.

Conditions That Support Teachers' Observation of the Lesson

Sometimes when teachers observe lessons, they are not sure what they should be looking for. Should they watch the students? the teacher? both? At other times when teachers observe lessons, they get involved by probing for more conversation during partner talk, conferring with students during independent reading or writing, or helping students with their work in some way. Their teaching tendencies come out and they want to teach. But the purpose of observing is to observe the decision-making process and to watch how the lesson is affecting the students and what the teacher is doing in response to the feedback the students are giving. If the observing teachers get involved with helping the students make sense of the lesson, not only are they no longer watching what the coach and teacher are doing, but they are also affecting the outcome of the lesson and making it impossible for the group to truly analyze the lesson as a whole.

Establish Guidelines About Communication with Students ◆ Explain to observing teachers why they should not interfere with the natural flow of the lesson (for example, by helping students with their writing or probing for more during partner talk) because the goal is to observe and analyze the lesson. Communicating with students for clarifying purposes is encouraged (for example, to ask a student to speak louder).

Establish Clear Expectations for the Students ◆ Let students know why they were selected to participate in the lesson, why the teachers are observing the lesson, and what they can expect during the lesson, and answer any questions they may have. Explain that the observing teachers are especially interested in hearing what they have to say and encourage them to speak loudly.

Establish Clear Expectations About What People Should Be Looking for in the Lesson ◆ During the set-up of the lesson, discuss what observers should be looking for. Sometimes you may want to guide the observation and other times the observers may decide on the observation. You can use the open-ended Lesson "Look For" Sheet (Figure 5–4) or a more specific observation protocol like the Sample Lesson Observation Protocol (Figure 5–5).

Establish Where Observing Teachers Should Be During the Lesson ◆ Observing teachers should not be clustered together in the back of the room, away from the action of the lesson. Instead, they should be as close as possible to where they need to be. Once the purpose of the observation is established in the set-up of the lesson, discuss where the observing teachers should be. For example, if the purpose is to look at conferring, the observing teachers need to gather around the student and teacher during the conference. If the purpose is to learn how to listen to student talk and make decisions based on student comments, the observing teachers need to walk alongside the teacher

Date _____   Time/Period/Class _____   Approach _____

During the lesson, gather information about:

_____

_____

_____

_____

NOTES:

FIG. 5–4 Lesson "Look For" Sheet

- We agreed to observe the lesson in triads.

- Prior to the lesson, assign roles to each member of the triad.
  - ☐ Who will script **TEACHER QUESTIONS?**
  - ☐ Who will script **STUDENT RESPONSES?**
  - ☐ Who will list **TEACHER MOVES?**

- After the lesson, use your scripts to determine the following:
  - ☐ What did the teacher do to support student engagement?
  - ☐ What did the teacher model?
  - ☐ How did the students share in the meaning making?
  - ☐ When were students practicing reading strategies on this text that can be used on another text?

© 2006 by Katherine Casey from *Literacy Coaching*. Portsmouth, NH: Heinemann.

FIG. 5–5 Sample Lesson Observation Protocol

and listen in. Yes, it is awkward moving around the classroom together as a group. But students adapt quickly, especially when we let them know why we are doing what we're doing, and adults adapt as they experience the value of seeing and hearing what is happening in the moment-by-moment decision making of a lesson.

Debriefing the Lesson

Reserve enough time to debrief the lesson so that observing teachers have opportunities to reflect on the lesson. If there are student work samples, provide teachers with time to analyze them. Provide opportunities for teachers to ask questions, make suggestions about how the lesson could be revised to be more even more effective, consider implications for their own work, clarify their understanding, and plan next steps.

 # Intravisitations and Intervisitations

Making our practice public can be a powerful tool in the improvement of instruction. By opening our classroom doors, we learn about best practices from colleagues whose students are achieving at high levels. A common question from teachers is, "Where can I go to see this happening?" Teachers want to observe in classrooms where work is happening and, no matter how thoughtfully you plan and teach them, watching you demonstrate a lesson is not the same as observing a teacher who works with students day in and day out—unless, of course, you are a teacher leader who still teaches your own class daily. Intravisitations are visits teachers make to their colleagues' classrooms within their school. Intervisitations are visits teachers make to another school.

Visitation Guidelines

Because visitations occur during the school day, you first need to determine how to arrange time for teachers to visit other classrooms. If the teacher needs to miss instructional time, who will cover the class? Resist the temptation to step in and do it yourself. For a visitation to be a purposeful and collaborative aspect of your coaching work (and not just an enjoyable opportunity to spend time in a colleague's classroom), you need to be a part of the visit. These guidelines should help your visitations be purposeful.

Establish a Clear Purpose ◆ As always when arranging a professional development opportunity, it is vital to establish a clear purpose and outcome for the visit. What do you and your teachers want to know and be able to do as a result of the visit? What do the visiting teachers need to see during the visit? What will they be expected to do with the learning that results from the visit?

Determine Which Teacher or Teachers to Visit ◆ Based on the purpose of the visit, determine which teacher or teachers you will visit. This takes some matchmaking and networking. By having one-on-one conversations with your teachers, observing teaching and learning in their classrooms, and having conversations with your principal, you have gathered a great deal of information about teachers' strengths and areas of need. Which teachers have *you* observed teaching in a way your teachers will benefit from seeing? Which students are learning in a way your teachers will benefit from seeing? Your principal or other colleagues may recommend visiting a teacher you haven't yet observed. I strongly recommend that you visit the recommended teacher's classroom *before* you take a group of teachers to observe. First, since you know the needs of your teachers and the context of your work with them, you will want to observe the recommended teacher's classroom to make sure the teaching and learning addresses your teachers' needs. Second, if you decide to arrange a visitation, you'll want to begin to establish a relationship with the host teacher before you arrive with a crowd. Third, you may want to take pictures of the room environment—with permission from the host teacher, of course—to share with your teachers before your visit so that they spend their observation time observing the teaching and learning. If you are planning an intervisitation to another school, make sure you contact the principal *before* contacting the potential host teacher to explain the purpose of your visit and to ask permission. Or your principal may want to contact the host teacher's principal to arrange the visit.

Communicate with the Host Teacher About the Purpose of the Visitation ◆ Make time to have a conversation with the host teacher about why you want to bring a group of teachers to visit her classroom. Ensure that the teacher is comfortable with your visit and will be engaged in the teaching and learning you want your teachers to see during the scheduled time. I like to be as explicit as possible about the purpose of my visit so that the host teacher is aware of what I hope for my teachers to see. For example, I recently brought a seventh-grade team to another school during writing workshop to see how collaboratively the students support each other in the writing process. When I explained the purpose to the host teacher, she reminded me that some of the scaffolds she put in place to support collaboration may be invisible at this point and suggested that we talk to a couple of her students during our prebrief about how they learned to be so collaborative. The teacher also made available some of the charts from earlier in the year that directly addressed how to be collaborative. Thank goodness I had a conversation with the host teacher, because without talking to her students and seeing the charts, our visit would have fallen short of our purpose.

Find out what the students have been working on lately and whatever you can about the students as learners to share with your teachers. You may also want to ask:

◆ Where do you prefer visiting teachers to gather during your lesson?
◆ What do you expect to be working on when we visit?
◆ Will you be available to talk with the group before and/or after the observation?

Hold a Previsitation Meeting ◆ Meet together as a group to reestablish the purpose of the visitation. Share with the teachers what the host teacher is working on with her students and what she expects them to observe. Create and distribute a "Look For" Sheet (Figure 5–4) to focus the observation. Encourage teachers to jot down questions as they observe. Whenever possible, have the host teacher join you to meet the visiting teachers and briefly review what visiting teachers will see.

Maximize the Visitation Time ◆ Make the most of your time observing in the teacher's classroom by arriving and settling in quickly. If the host teacher agreed that visitors are permitted to circulate, speak with students, and look at student materials, encourage teachers to do so. Remind them to take notes on the instruction and the classroom environment using the "Look For" Sheet.

Debrief After the Visitation ◆ Spend time discussing the observation and answering questions. If the host teacher can join the debrief, encourage the teachers to talk about the observation with the host teacher. I usually ask a question to focus the conversation on addressing the teacher's decision-making process: What did you learn about your students today that will help you plan for future lessons? Since the purpose of a visitation is to affect your teachers' instruction, it is helpful to brainstorm implications for everyone's work. Giving the host and visiting teachers an opportunity to reflect on and evaluate the day can help you shape future visitations.

◆ What did you take away from today's visit that you will use in your teaching?
◆ How could visitation process be improved for the next visit?
◆ What do you have questions about?
◆ What more do you need for your learning?

Follow Up the Visitation with the Host Teacher and the Visiting Teachers ◆ After a visitation, follow up with a thank-you note to the host teacher and, in the case of an intervisitation, to the host principal. As a teacher who was visited frequently, I cherished the thank-you notes I received from visitors because even if we had a chance to debrief together, I always wondered whether the visitors got something out of their visit. I also appreciated the recognition that hosting a visitation involves time and effort. Here is a letter from one visiting coach:

Katherine,

The fifth-grade teachers and I want to thank you for welcoming us into your classroom during writing workshop. Watching you model how to consider the counterarguments and then seeing your students work together to brainstorm possible counterarguments for their persuasive pieces sparked a lively conversation among my teachers about the writing process. We especially appreciate your students' willingness to explain to us how they chose their topics and what they want to accomplish by writing persuasive essays.

Thanks again for opening the doors of your classroom to us.

Sincerely,
Roxanne, literacy coach

Also, follow up with your teachers. You may want to send an email with a summary of the visit, especially the implications you brainstormed and any next steps you may be considering:

To: Fifth-grade team
From: Roxanne
Re: Visitation follow-up

Hi Team,

Thanks for your participation in yesterday's visit to Katherine's fifth-grade class. I appreciate your willingness to spend time away from your students to further our learning about the writing process. Based on our conversation and your feedback, we have some next steps as a group:

- We want to figure out how to shift away from giving students topics to having them select their own topics to write about.
- We liked how students gave each other feedback and want to try having students establish writing partnerships.
- We need to refer to the writing standards to make sure our lessons are grade-level appropriate.
- Two of us are going to try the counterargument lesson because we're in the midst of a persuasive unit.

And our questions:

- How would partnerships look throughout the writing process?
- What do we do when students say they have nothing to write about?
- How do we find grade-level exemplars of student writing to see if our students' work is good enough? (I think I found a good resource for you and am ordering a copy.)

I look forward to meeting with you next week during our grade-level planning time.

Thanks again for yesterday.

Teachers Arranging Intravisitations

As part of ongoing professional inquiry groups and lesson study, teachers may want to arrange informal visitations to colleagues' classrooms to observe teaching and learning without your involvement. These more informal visitations should also have a clear purpose connected to the teachers' ongoing work; engage teachers in teaching, assessing, observing, and reflecting; and aim toward achieving specific outcomes for both the host teacher and visiting teachers. Together with your principal, you and your teachers may find it helpful to cocreate expectations for intravisitations so that everyone involved sees the power of using visitation time to further teaching and learning. Figure 5–6 is an example of a intravisitation protocol a high school team created and used

Host Teacher: Josephine	Visiting Teacher(s): Renaldo
Date: 11/12	Period(s): sixth period (tenth-grade literature)

Purpose for the visit: I wanted to watch Josephine do a minilesson she talked about in our inquiry group last week that involved helping students get familiar with unfamiliar authors. Her students and mine seem reluctant to go outside their comfort zones when selecting independent reading texts.

What was observed:	Wonderings/ Thoughts:
I observed Josephine gather the students in the meeting area where she had unfamiliar texts arranged on her whiteboard ledge. She asked if any of the students were familiar with the books, and everyone said no. Then Josephine showed them how she tries to get herself excited about reading unfamiliar books in three ways:	Students were fascinated by the Amazon.com part.
	Should we print out some of those pages and put them in some of the unfamiliar books in our libraries?
Reading the back matter (the blurb on the back any critic's quotes), thinking aloud about the plot, characters, etc., and curiosity about what the critics had to say.	Will this minilesson help any of the students get connected to unfamiliar authors?
Reading the front matter (excerpts from the text, more critic's quotes, the dedication).	
Doing a quick check on Amazon.com—Josephine put a printout about one of the books on an overhead and showed students how Amazon has "Customers who bought this book also bought," which helps spark interest if you've read any of those books, and "Editorial Reviews," and "Customer Reviews," which help introduce you to the texts.	

Implications: I think, as a team, we should try this strategy with our students who don't venture out of their comfort zones. I'm going to print out Amazon.com pages for a few books that I think certain students might like and try it with a small group of students. Seeing how Josephine's students appeared interested in the "Customer Reviews" section because they realized other readers, and perhaps other high school students, wrote those reviews. A couple asked if they could write reviews, too. I'd like to discuss my ideas with the department at our next meeting.

Attachments:
☑ Lesson Plan
☐ Texts/Materials
☑ Other Amazon.com pages

FIG. 5–6 Classroom visitation summary

Host Teacher:	Visiting Teacher(s):
Date:	Period(s):

Purpose for the visit:	

What was observed:	Wonderings/ Thoughts:

Implications

Attachments:
☐ Lesson Plan
☐ Texts/Materials
☐ Other _____

© 2006 by Katherine Casey from *Literacy Coaching*. Portsmouth, NH: Heinemann.

FIG. 5–7 Classroom visitation summary

to keep the literacy teachers, literacy coach, and principal informed of their intravisitation learning. Figure 5–7 is a blank summary sheet for use.

Purposeful Involvement While Observing Lessons

Getting teachers involved during an observation can be an effective form of professional development when it is planned and purposeful. Some teachers hesitate to try on new learning with their students and prefer to practice first with a colleague's class. Other teachers need to try things in the moment and thrive on the opportunity for immediate feedback. Drawing the observing teachers into teaching and working with students during the classroom coaching session can be powerful and beneficial for all concerned.

My first introduction to conferring during independent reading occurred when I observed my colleague, Nancy, as she worked with Donna Santman, our reading staff developer. Though Donna's coaching work was housed in Nancy's classroom, Donna expected all the observing teachers to participate in her coaching work. With us gathered around, Donna demonstrated conferring with Nancy's students a number of times. She then suggested that Nancy confer with the next few students. As Nancy conferred, Donna whispered questions and suggestions in Nancy's ear, and Nancy voiced them to her students. That way, Nancy led the conference guided by Donna. After Nancy had tried a few conferences, Donna suggested that I try the next conference. "Oh no, that's OK," I answered, startled, and feeling totally intimidated by the idea that Donna, Nancy, and another colleague would be watching my first attempts. "I'll practice with my own students next period," I insisted. Not missing a beat, Donna replied, "Of course you'll practice with your own students. But first, you'll try conferring here." She knew that if I didn't try it with her guidance I would likely be frustrated when my attempts didn't resemble Donna's or Nancy's or I'd revert to my usual practices in a conference. I tried dodging again, this time asking Donna if she'd model just one more time. "Nope," Donna replied, "I'll model for you as you go. I'll whisper suggestions when you seem to get stuck."

Reluctantly and nervously, I sat down with a student, my colleagues gathered around and Donna by my side. I began conferring, basically mimicking what I had heard and seen Donna and Nancy do. Amazingly, the student responded intelligently, which threw me off because I didn't know what do with his smart responses. When Donna whispered a suggestion my ear, though I wanted desperately to get up and insist she finish the conference, I repeated her words to the student. Again, and not put off by the tag-team approach, the student revealed more of himself as a reader, and this time I knew what I wanted to say. Donna stood by me for the whole conference—which seemed to last an eternity—whispering in when I looked to her for help. Of course, she suggested I try a second conference and again whispered in when I got stuck. By the end of the second conference, I found my own voice and rhythm. Despite the barriers I threw in the path, Donna guided me to success, and the confidence and excitement I felt energized me to try conferring with my own students. Luckily we revisited conferring from time to time when Donna worked with us so that we could problem-solve and improve our skills.

Trying on conferring during independent reading or writing is not the only way to get observing teachers involved in trying on decision making. Think about what your teachers, both lead and observing, need for their learning. Then think about whether having a particular teacher actively participate in a portion of a lesson would further the teachers' learning.

Push Pause

Another way to purposefully involve observing teachers is to use a method I call *push pause* coaching. Prior to using this technique, I let observing teachers know that they should be prepared to participate in an aspect of the lesson. At the beginning of the lesson I let the students know that from time to time, I'm going to say, "Students, we're going to push pause on our work for a moment while I talk with the teachers." I explain, "During the pause you are expected to wait quietly, thinking about what you've just learned or what you'd like to say next, or perhaps stopping and jotting in your notebooks, while I talk to the teachers. When the lesson resumes, it may be me or an observing teacher or both of us leading the work."

I choose my push pause moments strategically, based on the teachers' ongoing work with me. For example, if how to use student ideas to grow a conversation is our focus, I may pause after hearing a series of student ideas. Or if how to model based on assessed student needs is our focus, I may pause right after discovering students need more support in making meaning of the text.

When I pause I might:

◆ Think aloud about my teaching decisions, explaining what I just did or am about to do and why: "Teachers, did you see how I just had the students rehearse their writing ideas aloud before sending them off to independent writing? I did that because I want us to see if having the students rehearse their ideas helps them get started on their writing more effectively and efficiently. Please help me watch how the students get started writing in just a minute."

◆ Highlight what just happened in the lesson, commenting on what students just did: "Teachers, did you see how the students used ideas from last week's series of minilessons about how to gather ideas across texts to be more critical of the ideas in this text?"

◆ Ask for suggestions about what to do next and then try the suggestion and have the participants watch the results.

◆ Request that an observing teacher take the lead for a moment in order to give the teacher an opportunity to try something on: "Students, I'm going to push pause for a moment because I'd like Ms. Kozai to ask you a few follow-up questions."

◆ Ask for help when I get stuck: "Teachers, I'm not sure where to go from here. What do you recommend?"

 ## Lesson Study

Developed in Japan by mathematics teachers, lesson study is a professional development process that engages educators in systematically examining their instructional practice with the goal of becoming more effective. The lesson study cycle involves professional inquiry and study, collaborative lesson planning, observations of colleagues teaching the co-planned lessons while others collect data, reflection after the observation, and then the cycle begins again. Lesson study can be an appropriate and highly effective ongoing professional development structure for your group of teachers. Hurd and Licciardo-Musso's (2005) article on the use of lesson study for literacy instruction offers a clear explanation of how lesson study works and will give you many ideas to consider.

It is crucial to bring teachers together to problem-solve a common instructional need so that everyone is invested in the process. Here's the process I use when I engage a team of teachers in lesson study.

◆ **Study** The teachers, most often a grade-level team or department, and I meet to discuss our students' strengths and areas of need, standards, and curriculum. We work collaboratively to a clear picture of what our students need for their learning and what we want them to know and be able to do as a result of our work.

◆ **Plan** Together, we co-plan a lesson. We determine both what to teach and how to teach, getting specific about the materials, what might go on charts, guiding questions and prompts, anticipating times the teacher may need to model and scaffold the learning, what students are going to be expected to try on, what student understanding may look like and sound like, and so on.

◆ **Teach** We watch our colleague teach our co-planned lesson to determine what students know and are able to do as a result of the lesson and how it needs to be revised to better meet the needs of the students. When I work with a group of new teachers or with a group of experienced teachers who are new to the work, the group often wants me to teach the first lesson for two major reasons: even though they co-planned the lesson, they can't envision how the lesson might look; or, the teachers are reluctant to teach in front of their colleagues and want to see how the process works before taking a risk.

◆ **Reflect and Replan**   We engage in private reflection and group discussion of the lesson and make revisions to the lesson.

◆ **Teach**   A second colleague teaches the revised lesson and the cycle of observation, reflection, and revision repeats.

◆ **Apply**   Finally, teachers agree to try the lesson with their students, decide which artifacts of learning and teaching to gather, and return in the next few days with their revised lesson plans and artifacts to discuss their experiences. These discussions lead to additional instructional implications and propel forward a cycle of professional inquiry, problem solving, discovery, application, revision, and improvement.

I lead a condensed lesson study in one day (Figure 5–8) or over two to three consecutive days, depending entirely on how much time we have for our professional development. I encourage you to consider the possibilities of lesson study in short bursts and over time, based, as always, on the short-term and long-term needs of your teachers and their students.

 ## Co-planning Lessons

There never seems to be enough time for lesson planning, and teachers appreciate and benefit from co-planning lessons when the time devoted to it is well-structured and relevant to them. The benefit of co-planning occurs when together teachers create lessons that are more effective than the ones they create on their own. Co-planning does not mean each teacher plans a few lessons that others copy; nor does it mean gathering together in the same room to plan lessons individually. Co-planning lessons involves a thoughtful process that usually takes more time than a teacher devotes on a daily basis to lesson planning. By slowing down the planning process and encouraging everyone to carefully consider every part of the lesson—student strengths and areas of need as identified through examination of student work and formal and informal assessment data, what students need next for their learning, what students

Time	Purpose	Materials/Location	Outcome
8:15–9:00	Study: • What are our students' strengths? • What are our students' areas of need? • Which standards are we addressing? • Which curriculum expectations are we addressing?	Conferring notes, anecdotal records, student work, and any other relevant artifacts. *Coach's room*	Build a clear picture of the students we are planning for.
9:00–9:50	Plan: Co-plan a lesson based on what students need for their learning. Let's figure out: • What students should know and be able to do • How we will get them there • Materials • Prompts/questions • Anticipated scaffolds • What they'll try on • Checking for understanding Let's also get clear about what we will be researching during the lesson.	Grade-level-appropriate narrative texts connected to short story unit. *Coach's room*	Create a solid lesson plan. Create a solid plan for researching during the lesson.
9:50–10:00	Transition to Teacher No. 1's room		
10:00–10:30	Teach/research: Observe the co-planned lesson with the research questions in mind. • What is supporting the student learning? • What are students learning and how do we know? • What more do students need for their learning?	Observation forms Name tags for students *Teacher No. 1's room*	Analyze our lesson in action to determine what worked, why, how we know, and what needs revision.
10:30–10:45	Break		

FIG. 5–8 One-day lesson study schedule (*reading of narrative texts*)

10:45– 11:45	Reflect and replan: • Privately reflect, examine student work (either actual work or scripts of student talk), and organize for share • Lesson teacher—reflect, comment on lesson strengths, decisions made, surprises, evidence of lesson goals met • Group share—significant observations and implications Lesson Revision—What did we learn from the first attempt that can help strengthen the second attempt?	Observation notes Scripts of student and teacher talk Student work, charts, any other artifacts *Coach's room*	Determine what worked, why, how we know, and what needs revision.
11:45– 12:30	Lunch		
12:30– 1:00	Teach/research: Observe the co-planned lesson with the research questions in mind. • What is supporting the student learning? • What are students learning and how do we know? • What more do students need for their learning? • What affect are our revisions having on student learning?	Observation forms Name tags for students *Teacher No. 2's room*	Analyze the revisions we made to our lesson to determine what worked, why, how we know, and what needs revision.
1:30– 2:15	Reflect and replan: • Privately reflect, examine student work (either actual work or scripts of student talk), and organize for share • Lesson teacher—reflect, comment on lesson strengths, decisions made, surprises, evidence of lesson goals met • Group share—significant observations and implications Lesson revision—What did we learn from the second attempt that can help strengthen the third attempt?	Observation notes Scripts of student and teacher talk Student work, charts, any other artifacts *Coach's room*	Determine what worked, why, how we know, and what needs revision.

Continues

Time	Purpose	Materials/Location	Outcome
2:15–2:45	Apply: Based on the two lessons we worked on today, what are the implications for upcoming lessons in our classrooms? Use this time to tweak the co-planned lesson for your own students. Teachers 1 and 2, plan for follow-up lessons to today's lesson.	Lesson plans for the next few days *Coach's room*	Revise or create lesson plans that reflect our work together.
2:45–3:00	Evaluate: Reflect on today's learning and evaluate both the structure and the content of the day.	Evaluation sheet *Coach's room*	Determine how to improve the lesson study process.

FIG. 5–8 Cont.

should know and be able to do as a result of the lesson, what materials to use, how to scaffold the learning, what visuals are needed, what students will try on, and how the teacher will check for understanding—teachers experience the decision-making process of designing effective lessons. With practice, and as the thought processes become internalized, the planning process speeds up.

I recommend that co-planning lessons happen *after* teachers have observed instruction together and not before. I used to engage teachers in co-planning lessons early in our work together because I thought co-planning lessons and modeling my thinking about the decisions I make in my lesson planning and encouraging teachers to share their decision-making processes would help all of us in our teaching. After a number of failed attempts, I realized that co-planning fell short because, though we had agreed to co-plan a lesson, each of us had quite a different image of what a lesson should look and sound like. Now when I consider using co-planning as a professional development structure, I ask myself, "If I were to ask each teacher in the planning group to describe her vision of the type of lesson we're trying to plan, what would each teacher picture?" Before launching into co-planning lessons, I want to be sure that the group has at least the beginning of a common vision so that we are working together toward a common goal. I attach co-planning to other professional development structures that help teachers build a common vision of lessons. For example, after observing a videotaped lesson or demonstration lesson, or as part of lesson study or coaching cycles, teachers can co-plan what the next lesson or series of lessons would involve or could plan lessons similar to the lessons they viewed together.

 ## Attending Professional Development Conferences

Teachers need opportunities to leave their building, their district, and even their state or country to broaden and deepen their professional knowledge and skill, to network with fellow educators, to become aware of innovative practices, to recharge, to be inspired—and all of these opportunities can be made possible by attending professional development conferences.

I regularly get fliers in the mail promoting professional development conferences, announcing featured leaders in our field, describing wonderful, even indulgent-sounding professional opportunities ("Spend a day with nationally noted authors who will model exemplary teaching strategies with children," read one and "Work alongside fellow primary teachers developing practical learning experiences for your students" read another). And I want to attend, not just to learn how to become a better teacher, but to meet new educators, learn about what's working for their students, and to enjoy collegial study.

In my own career some of the most profound learning I've done has happened at professional conferences, especially those that stretch across a series of days and provide opportunities to not only learn about powerful instruction, but also experience it firsthand. I've attended one-day workshops, too, that opened my eyes to instructional practices I just had to get back to my school to try with my students.

But, you ask, hasn't job-embedded professional development, like your job as a literacy coach, evolved, in large part, because attending professional development conferences has not proven effective in improving teaching and learning? For years, research has supported what most educators already knew: that one-shot workshops or training opportunities without follow-up or immediate relevance to teacher needs do not impact teacher practice or student learning (Joyce and Showers 1988). Looking carefully at the research, it sounds to me like attending the conference isn't the issue; follow-up and immediate relevance are.

So let's unite professional development conferences with the wisdom from the research—sessions need to be immediately relevant and teachers need follow-up—to provide teachers with professional development opportunities that cannot occur in our own buildings but that can, with our support, spark lasting and effective instructional changes.

Start with relevance. Seek out conferences that connect to the work you and your teachers are doing together and encourage your teachers to do the same. Get on the mailing list of professional organizations such as IRA and NCTE. Check out professional text publisher websites. Pay attention to advertisements within professional journals and local education newsletters. When you hear about a conference, try to determine to what degree the purpose is aligned with your ongoing work with teachers. Research the qualifications of the presenter or organization. You may have to do additional research by calling or emailing conference organizers to find out what the conference involves and to determine what you can expect your teachers will know and be able to do as a result of attending the conference.

Are all your teachers excited to attend, or at least enough of them to inspire the others? No point in sending teachers to a conference that does not interest them and isn't immediately relevant to their teaching. Attending conferences as a team is vital and far more enjoyable than school-based professional development. You want a team of teachers sharing a common experience so that they can support each other when they bring back the ideas and implement them in their classrooms. You'll have to attend the conference with your teachers so that you can learn alongside them and so that you can help sustain the work back at school. Invite your principal to attend, too.

Plan for follow-up. How *will* you provide teachers with opportunities for ongoing support? Some conferences provide ongoing learning opportunities in the weeks and months following the conference. If not, schedule follow-up sessions at school for your teachers. You don't have to have all the answers for what that follow-up will look like, you just need to reserve the time with your teachers. When I attend conferences with teachers, we meet for coffee or breakfast before the session to talk about our expectations for the day. Though we are usually exhausted, we meet after the session for an hour to discuss implications for our work, jot lists of things to remember to talk more about, materials we may need to purchase, and our ideas for next steps. I use those meetings to make note of the type of follow-up it seems my teachers need for their learning. Even if the principal has not been able to attend the conference, I invite the principal to join our debrief meeting to get a feel for

FIG. 5–9 A school-based professional development session

the learning we've engaged in together and the implications for our teaching and learning.

 ## Joining in Professional Inquiry Groups

Professional inquiry groups foster a collaborative culture among teachers, which is strongly linked to improving schools (DuFour, Eaker, and DuFour 2005). Creating structures that ensure collaboration helps combat the teacher isolation that schools foster. Inquiry groups enable small groups of teachers with a common need to come together to pursue knowledge and skill or to accomplish a common goal focused on the improvement of teaching and learning. Groups focus on problem-solving specific problems of practice and together they build communities of practice.

Participation in an inquiry group may be self-selected or can be organized by you, always around commonalities among the participants. Often literacy coaches help get the initial group structure started, and then, over time, the groups become self-sustaining.

Teams of teachers might form to assess student work, to observe students at work, to research and select instructional materials, or to design curriculum based on specific learning outcomes and student needs. Groups might form to engage in peer observation and peer coaching, or to develop benchmarks and assessments aligned with standards. Groups might form to read and discuss children's literature or might study professional texts, to apply the ideas to their work with students, and to evaluate the effectiveness of the work.

Often the need for inquiry groups arises as a staff learns together and realizes that teachers have different areas of interest and need within the school's focus. For example, an elementary school working on implementing writer's workshop might have groups of teachers pursuing various questions like: How *does* interactive writing support emergent writers in the writing process? What supports do English Language Learners need for their learning? What does exemplary student writing look like at each grade level? What mentor texts can we use in upper grades? How do we grade student writing?

What they learn together can spark inquiry groups to design and facilitate professional development for the colleagues who can benefit from the knowledge. The mentor text team, for example, might create collections of texts for the entire grade level while the members of the team that focused on grading might lead a session on grading student writing for their colleagues. In this way, inquiry groups promote collaboration and knowledge and skill building not only within the team, but across teams as well.

Time can be one of the barriers to getting the most from professional inquiry groups. Professional inquiry requires opportunities to learn over time, have conversations, go off to classrooms to experiment and work with students, read more, return to the group for more discussion, and so on. Consider situating professional inquiry groups within existing professional development structures—as a portion of a whole-staff conference, during a grade-level or department meeting, or for the last hour of an intravisitation day, for example.

Another barrier for participants can be staying focused on the tasks at hand. A side effect of being isolated from adults for most of the day is that when teachers do gather, there is so much to talk about that staying focused on professional inquiry can be challenging. As you work with teachers in professional inquiry groups, the group may need to establish norms and expectations. The success of professional inquiry groups rests not on your facilitation or the protocol you create, but in each member's commitment to the inquiry work itself.

Developing methods of communication among various teams can help share the wealth. A large bulletin board in a staff room with space for inquiry teams to post recent learning, periodic emails to colleagues, or brief announcements during staff meetings can help colleagues stay informed. If inquiry groups are a popular professional development structure within your school, you will not be able to be a member of every inquiry group, yet you will want to know what teams are learning. Some literacy coaches ask inquiry teams to email a brief update each time they meet, and then the literacy coach compiles an update for the staff.

 ## Videotaping and Analyzing Lessons

There is nothing more eye-opening than watching a videotape of yourself teaching. Once you get past the initial shock of how you look and sound, and groan about your outfit or hairstyle or mannerisms or how you're aging, analyzing your own instructional practice gives you a perspective you just cannot have as you teach—the perspective of watching how you interact with students and what you *actually* say and do, as opposed to what you *think* you say and do. And this perspective can transform teaching and learning in subtle and powerful ways. By watching myself on video I realized:

- I had strengths I wasn't aware of—like ample wait time, trying to teach for understanding, and connecting current learning to prior and future learning.

- Many times I wasn't actually teaching what I thought I was teaching. Depending on the lesson, my purpose was unclear, I didn't check for understanding enough, my modeling went on too long, or not long enough, or my students asked questions I didn't understand or value so I glossed over them.

- When I made a concerted effort to assimilate feedback colleagues gave me, my teaching became more focused and more supportive of my students' needs.

- My questions were not clear. Before having students talk, I'd ask three or four slightly different versions of the same question. Why? Because I thought I didn't need to carefully plan my lessons, that I could go with the flow and spontaneously ask the right questions. The videotape showed me how my muddled language confused the students and justified why I needed to be more thoughtful in my lesson planning.

◆ Certain students, usually the students closer to me and in my direct line of vision, dominated the lessons. Many students rarely spoke.

◆ The big ideas I thought we were addressing weren't that big. Lots of the student talk was repetitive and students weren't challenging each other's ideas.

◆ My lessons didn't have much closure because we ran out of time. Rather than spend a few minutes summarizing the work of the day by stating what we accomplished, our work ended with statements like, "Quickly, students, get ready for lunch," or "Put your independent reading away, let's go, we've got to move into writing workshop."

Analyzing my videotapes made me aware of the coaching and ongoing professional development opportunities I needed to take advantage of in order to improve. My professional life is videotaped—the lessons I teach, the professional development sessions I lead for teachers and coaches, even the planning meetings I have with district leaders—and I spend time analyzing the tapes. I still wince when I watch myself, but I can say with certainty that without videotaping and analyzing my work, I cannot get gain the perspective I need to improve my practice.

How can you use videotaping in your coaching work? Begin by getting the right equipment because without it, the videotape will be useless. The basics include the video camera, a tripod, and most important, a wireless microphone. I recommend either a wireless clip-on microphone or a shotgun microphone that sits on a table or in the middle of the group of students. You must be able to hear what you and the students are saying during the lesson. Before suggesting to teachers that they might want to videotape themselves, videotape yourself. No need to ask someone to videotape you. Instead, set up the camera on the tripod far enough away so that you can see you and the students; pop in a blank, rewound tape; double-check to make sure the microphone is working; and push record. After the lesson, watch yourself and analyze your own instruction, just as you might analyze your teachers' lessons.

Here are some effective ways to introduce the use of videotape:

◆ Schedule time to videotape two lessons. After watching the first lesson, list your strengths and areas of need, create an action plan, and commit to trying to make changes to your instructional practice in the second lesson. Videotape your second lesson, making the instructional changes. You can either tape yourself teaching the same group of students to show how you adjusted your second lesson to better meet the students' needs, or you can tape yourself teaching a different group of students, applying what you learned by analyzing your first lesson. To model the use of videotape as a way to engage in reflective practice, share your first video with teachers and have them analyze your instruction. Together, establish norms about how to analyze lessons and what kind of feedback is helpful. Compare their analysis with yours and emphasize how helpful it is to have the feedback of a group of educators. Show the second lesson, have teachers observe you trying to improve your own instruction, and then discuss their observations. By using your own videos, you not only model reflective practice, you show your teachers that you are willing to put your own practice out for the benefit of the group, and you set the stage for teachers to videotape themselves.

◆ Ask your principal or individual teachers if they would be willing to help you analyze a video. Explain that you value their perspective and benefit from hearing their feedback. Analyzing lessons together can help establish trust and common understanding of effective instruction.

◆ Use videotape in conjunction with lesson study or co-planning lessons. When teachers have ownership in the creation of a lesson, they are more curious as they watch the video. Volunteer to videotape yourself teaching the co-planned lesson and suggest that the group meet together to analyze the lesson. Over time, encourage others to videotape themselves and have the group analyze their lessons.

◆ Sometimes the hassle of getting the equipment together stifles a teacher's enthusiasm for videotaping. Offer to set up the camera in a teacher's room for her private use.

Go Beyond Videotaping Lessons

Be creative with your use of videotaping. In addition to using it for lesson analysis, here's how one district used video to find the answers to some pertinent questions:

◆ *Are our libraries organized for student access?* The district spent a great deal of money and effort organizing classroom libraries and teaching students how to use the libraries, and teachers wanted to know if their efforts were paying off. I asked teachers to select students about whom they had concerns during independent reading. I told the small group of students that I needed their help figuring out how to make classroom libraries even easier to use, and that my question for them to answer on video was, "If a child from another class came into your classroom and asked you how your library works, what would you say?" After school I videotaped the students, explaining the organization of the library, and prompted them to offer ways to make the classroom library easier to use. At a whole-staff conference, I showed photographs of libraries and clips of students from each grade level talking about their classroom libraries. The students' feedback opened our eyes to ideas we had not considered and dramatically shifted how we organized libraries for student access.

◆ *What do proficient readers think about as they read?* This question guided a middle school's professional inquiry group. To help answer the question, teachers decided to have students who scored at the proficient level on the state reading standards test read a somewhat challenging piece of text and talk about their thinking on camera. The teachers selected a common text and agreed to tape two students per class. Viewing and analyzing ten proficient students sparked curiosity and led to additional inquiry questions and lists of possible reading lessons to teach.

◆ *What does teaching for meaning look like and sound like?* The primary teachers kept wondering what it really looks like and sounds like to make meaning of books written for children younger than third grade. They agreed to videotape themselves having conversations about books written by Jan Brett, Cynthia Rylant, and Eric Carle to see what they talked about. They also videotaped small groups of children talking about the same texts during interactive read-aloud. Teachers experimented with the instructional strategies they read about in professional texts and videotaped lessons to study together.

◆ *Do we make effective use of our time?* After growing frustrated by not getting much done during their grade-level planning time, and trying without much success to problem-solve how to be more efficient, two teachers wondered aloud, "Where does our time go?" The grade-level team of six teachers agreed, some reluctantly, to videotape and analyze their next grade-level planning session. Their analysis helped them prioritize what they wanted to accomplish together, craft a streamlined agenda for future planning sessions that balanced time to vent with time to plan, and increased productivity and goodwill among the team.

Supporting Your Teachers

So are you any closer to figuring out how, exactly, you plan to support your teachers and their students' needs? All eight ways of studying instruction can provide powerful learning opportunities that begin to change teacher practice. Watching you and others demonstrating lessons, visiting other classrooms, and being purposefully involved in observation help teachers envision the possibilities. Being part of a lesson study, during which we can slow down, collaboratively revise, and reteach a lesson until it starts to actually work for students, satisfies our desire to get it right. Professional conferences inspire us. Analyzing videotaped lessons lets us see ourselves from our students' vantage point. Collaborating with colleagues in inquiry groups or as we co-plan lessons creates opportunities for us to pool our collective knowledge toward meeting students' needs. Which supports make sense for your teachers and students?

Models of Intensive
Classroom Support

There comes a time in our coaching work when must get into teachers' classrooms and personally work with them, one-on-one, day after day, to support their professional development. To be sure, the ways to study instruction in Chapter 5 allow teachers to grapple with instructional decision making in real-life ways. But none provide what we often wish we had: someone to work with us every day, reaching out to help us when we just don't know what to do, demonstrating techniques that work with our students right then and there, encouraging us to tolerate the awkwardness of reinventing ourselves—especially when it is a lot easier to fall back on old, comfortable habits.

Two models of intensive classroom support—the gradual release coaching cycle and the unit of study coaching cycle—are designed around the need to give teachers ongoing support over time in their classrooms. The time required varies depending on the teacher and students' needs, of course, but ideally involves at least five closely scheduled sessions for the gradual release cycle and once a week for the duration of the unit in the unit of study cycle. Though not easy, finding time to engage in a gradual release coaching cycle is possible, as Bethany Robinson, a literacy coach in the Highline School District in Washington, explains:

> To find time for gradual release coaching cycles, I look at my planner and highlight what I call the "prime literacy time," which is when my teachers teach reading and writing. I try to put my coaching cycles first on my calendar because the opportunities to work in classrooms with teachers and students during their literacy time is limited.

Because I find I need three to five days in a row with teachers to do a coaching cycle, I look at my month and try to find consecutive days. I used to think about days in a week and now I think about days in a row. For example, if I have Thursday, Friday, and then Monday, Tuesday, I can block that time for a four-day coaching cycle. Some of my teachers are fine with me working with them for two days, skip a day, and then back into their room again. So a Monday, Tuesday, and then Thursday, Friday, Monday span of time will work.

I regularly use both coaching cycle methods with brand-new as well as veteran K–12 teachers. What we learn together about students and ourselves is always enlightening and frequently profound. The models aren't quick fixes, nor are they easy. But then again, neither are teaching students and ensuring that all are learning day after day.

 ## Gradual Release Coaching Cycle

A gradual release coaching cycle is designed to provide teachers with side-by-side support in the classroom over a period of (ideally) consecutive days as teachers develop aspects of their teaching practice.

Developed by David Pearson and Maria Gallagher (1983), the gradual release of responsibility model begins with an emphasis on teacher modeling. In the first phase, students are exposed to ideas, skills, and strategies that they may not yet know and are not yet able to do independently. Students need plenty of opportunities to see an accomplished model (the teacher) interact with and make meaning of texts, communicate meaning in writing, and highlight the thinking that underpins doing a task well. The gradual release coaching cycle begins with an emphasis on the coach's modeling lessons and thinking aloud about the decisions she is making, so that the teacher experiences not just the lesson but also some of the in-the-moment decision-making strategies the coach is using.

The next phase involves students' trying on and experimenting with what the teacher has modeled. What the students are expected to know and be able to do needs to be within their zone of proximal development, of course. Multiple opportunities to practice and approximate are provided with appropriate feedback from the teacher and classmates as students move toward independence. The teacher needs to continually assess students to adjust the scaffolds students need to be successful. Scaffolds are meant to be temporary structures that help the students be successful something that would otherwise be quite challenging. For example, the teacher may need to model more explicitly, think aloud more often, modify the task to be less complex, provide more visual supports, and so on, based on what students need for their learning. Over time, the scaffolds should fade away as students become more able to do the work without as much teacher support.

Similarly, the next phase of coaching involves the teacher, who experiments with what the coach has modeled while the coach provides scaffolding based on the teacher's need. The coach's expectations must be within the teacher's zone of proximal development. Side-by-side teaching is the hallmark of this phase. The teacher and coach teach the lesson together after co-planning and anticipating the types of scaffolds the teacher may need during the lesson. Just as it is the teacher's responsibility to ensure that students feel supported, so is it the coach's responsibility to ensure that the teacher feels supported as she steps into unfamiliar and uncomfortable teaching territory. Being responsive to the students' and the teacher's needs and deciding which scaffolds to use and when are skills a coach develops with practice.

The final phase involves having students make decisions about what they need for their learning and successfully applying the skills and strategies they've learned independently. The temporary scaffolds fade away because the students are shored up with their own knowledge and skill. Independent does not necessarily mean alone. Instead, students are encouraged to use each other and, when necessary the teacher, for support. Similarly, in the final phase of the gradual release coaching model the teacher practices applying the skills and strategies she has learned, taking responsibility for the majority of the decision making within the lesson. The coach remains nearby for support, ready to assist the teacher if necessary.

What Is Side-by-Side Teaching?

Side-by-side teaching involves two teachers working as one in close proximity to each other to teach students. It is based on the premise that teachers benefit from guidance and the opportunity to discuss their teaching as they teach. Though we can learn by reading professional texts, watching instructional videos, planning lessons, and observing others, our knowledge only becomes skill when we actually teach students, and slowly gain mastery of our craft. Too often educators are expected to apply knowledge gained in professional development to their teaching without the immediate support of a colleague. Side-by-side teaching provides that necessary element.

Side-by-side teaching is not coteaching. Co-teaching has been defined as "the delivery of substantive instruction by two or more professionals to a diverse or blended group of students in a single space" (Cook and Friend 1995, 2), and often with each teacher taking responsibility for teaching a portion of the class. In side-by-side teaching, the coach and teacher take responsibility for aspects of the same lesson. Responsibility may shift back and forth between the coach and teacher, allowing the coach to model something the teacher can then practice. Or the coach may simply act as a guide, making suggestions, giving reminders, and offering encouragement as the teacher teaches. What the coach and teacher work on together and how they negotiate their roles depend on the teacher's needs.

Shifting Responsibility

Literacy coach Paul is working with ninth-grade teacher Claudia, who is frustrated because, despite her best efforts, she cannot seem to get her students to move beyond pat, literal responses about the ideas in texts. Her frustration increases when she watches Paul demonstrate a lesson in which the student responses far surpass her expectations. Because now she sees that her students are capable of better work, she concludes that her teaching is getting in the way. Paul suggests they side-by-side teach. Claudia will teach the bulk of the lesson with Paul sitting next to her, and he will step in when he sees opportunities to push the students' responses. After modeling a few times as the lesson progresses, Paul explains that rather than talk directly to the students, he will whisper suggestions to Claudia that she will voice to the students. Skeptical, but eager for a solution to her teaching dilemma, Claudia agrees to give it a try. From the students' perspective, it looks like tag-team teaching, and Paul's questioning and modeling intrigue them. Claudia has read about his techniques in professional texts and heard them discussed in meetings, but just can't seem to find the right words to try with her students because the language doesn't seem natural. Paul whispers to her to give it a try, Claudia looks at him, unsure, so Paul whispers, "Say 'In what ways are these characters projecting stereotypes?'" Claudia repeats his words to the class and the students appear eager to talk to their partners. As they do, Claudia mutters to Paul, "That worked! Give me some more things to say." The lesson continues with Paul whispering in and Claudia taking on new teaching techniques. During the debrief Claudia remarks that she knew in her head what to do and say but needed Paul to give her the words and make her say them. She asks if they could try it again with her next class, so that the seemingly unnatural language could become more comfortable for her.

Claudia's experience is one I've had many, many times. I study instruction, gather many terrific ideas from professional texts, and try the ideas on in my own teaching with various degrees of success. I feel awkward, like I am pretending to be someone else, which in a real sense, I am—I am trying to become a more effective version of myself. Then, more often than not, I either revert back to my more comfortable self, or erroneously think I'm doing it. Side-by-side teaching is a bridge between knowledge and skill that consistently helps teachers start to use effective strategies they can then practice and refine on their own.

Suggesting, Reminding, Encouraging

Fourth-grade teacher Antonio is part of an ongoing study group using a professional text about think-aloud strategies. He and his colleagues have watched each other teach and discovered that they either think aloud far too much, causing the students to lose interest, or not enough. Antonio is concerned that he may be stopping too frequently, interrupting the flow of text so much that he is inadvertently causing the students to lose meaning. His coach, Loran, has observed Antonio and sees validity in his concerns. She suggests they teach side-by-side. Loran explains that she will monitor her own ability to make meaning as Antonio reads, and, if he stops too soon, will signal him to continue. She will also help him monitor the students' needs, again signaling if he needs to adjust the amount of think-alouds. While Antonio teaches, Loran resembles an athletic coach, signaling, suggesting, and nodding. During the debrief Antonio shares that having Loran there as another set of eyes and ears helped him monitor and adjust his own teaching and gave him a level of awareness: "There's so much to think about during a lesson. Knowing that you were there to prompt me and help me through it made me feel as if I was teaching and watching myself teach through your eyes. By the end of the lesson, I could pretty much predict what you were going to suggest, and I think I started to develop a new set of instincts about thinking aloud."

Getting into the Lesson and Giving It Back

Teachers worry that in side-by-side teaching the coach is going to take over the lesson or that after the coach gets involved, the teacher won't know where to take the lesson. Be strategic about how to address both concerns.

Establish a Signal for Entry ◆ Both of you will need to discuss how you will get into the lesson when the other is teaching. What will be your signal for entry? How will you let the teacher know that you want to say something to the students or model something for the teacher? Here are signals some coaches use:

◆ I raise my hand, just as the students do, to let the teacher know I want to talk. The teacher either calls on me or, if she isn't ready for my participation, she says she'll call on me soon.

◆ I usually sit next to the teacher as she models writing or reading lessons standing at the overhead. When I start to stand up, she knows I want to participate.

◆ We sit next to each other as we teach. Usually just a lean toward the teacher is enough of a signal.

Similarly, when you are teaching, what is the teacher's signal for wanting to participate in what you're doing? Talk about it together and experiment until you find a system that works for you. The point of having the discussion and establishing a signal for entry is to help build a respectful relationship in which you acknowledge that even though the coaching relationship may make the teacher feel out of control, the teacher is still very much in control of the situation.

Talking about how the teacher will request your help is also useful. Some teachers worry that they won't know what to do when they are trying on new learning and want the reassurance that you, as coach, will step in and provide assistance. When the teacher is teaching and wants your help, what will the signal be? Here's what some teachers do:

◆ I look over at my coach and give her a pleading look, and she steps right in.

◆ I say to my students, "Let's see what Ms. Casey thinks."

◆ I like having those few moments to figure out how we're going to proceed next. I have my students turn and talk to each other so I have a minute to talk to my coach. Sometimes my coach just gives me a helpful suggestion. And sometimes I tell my coach I want her to do the next part of the lesson.

With practice, you and your teacher will develop a way of communicating during lessons that works for you and may not resemble what you decided in advance your signals will be. The purpose of having the discussion is to lessen anxiety by openly discussing how you will work together.

Give the Lesson Back ◆ I remember watching my coach jump into my lesson and worrying about what I would do when she wanted me to continue the lesson. My mind was flooded with thoughts like, "Where should I go next? What am I supposed to do now? I wish she would just teach the rest of the lesson." Why it never occurred to me to just ask my coach what I should do next, I don't know. Maybe I didn't want to look incompetent in front of my coach and students. My attention to explaining to the teacher before we side-by-side teach how I will transfer the lesson back to her stems from my own worry that the teacher will panic as I used to do.

I am explicit and deliberate when I give the lesson back to the teacher and use the students to help me do so. I explain to the students exactly what is going to happen next, ask them if they are clear on what will happen next, at which point the teacher usually realizes she is about to resume teaching, and, even if the students say they are clear, I repeat my explanation so that the teacher can hear me and get ready. I might say, "Students, I just modeled for you how I added more realism to our character sketch by adding movements and gestures. Ms. Alexander is going to show you how adding movements or gestures to our 'he said/she said' statements can add depth, too. For example, where we wrote, ' "Abigail, you betrayed me," accused Rebecca,' Ms. Alexander may have you add a gesture, like, 'accused Rebecca, dropping her head into her hands.' Are you ready, students? Ms. Alexander is going to work on this section of dialogue with you." By using the teacher's name and explaining what I just did and what the teacher is going to do next, I help the teacher get her mind back into the lesson so that she doesn't have to read my mind about where the lesson is going.

With practice, you will develop strategies for giving the lesson back to the teachers with whom you work, and you will base how explicit you need to be when giving the lesson back based on the teacher's needs.

How Long Does a Gradual Release Coaching Cycle Take?

The length of a gradual release coaching cycle varies, depending on what the teacher needs for her learning and how much time you have. The minimum is three closely spaced sessions to allow the gradual release of responsibility from modeling, to side-by-side teaching, to supported independence. Like students, adults don't learn in a linear fashion. So you might demonstrate a few times, do side-by-side teaching, and then need to demonstrate again, because you are responding to the teacher's needs. The five-session coaching cycle described in Figure 6–1 is meant to be one example of how you might release responsibility to the teacher over the course of a week. If you had ten days, you might double the amount of time you spend on each session, doing four demos instead of two; or you might repeat the five-session cycle twice; or you might spend six days teaching side-by-side. The key to the successful use of this model requires applying the gradual release theory to your teacher's needs within your time frame.

Preparing for Gradual Release Coaching Cycle

Whenever you prepare to coach a teacher, one with whom you have or have not yet worked, starting with a classroom observation is a wise idea because your observation will help you get a sense of the students' and teacher's strengths and needs and give you some insight into what students are currently learning. You may or may not already know that you intend to do a gradual release coaching cycle; it will depend on what the teacher needs. For example, you may realize the teacher would benefit more from coaching within a unit of study than from a gradual release coaching cycle. Here are some questions to consider.

Things to Consider During Your Observation

What are the students' strengths and needs?

What are the teacher's strengths and needs?
- What does the teacher expect the students to know and be able to do as a result of the lesson?
- How does the teacher introduce the purpose of the lesson?
- How does the teacher pace the lesson to allow for modeling and student involvement?
- What kinds of support does the teacher provide during the lesson?
- What questions is the teacher asking to support students in making meaning?
- How does the teacher manage the students?
- How does the teacher check for understanding and adjust the lesson to meet student needs?
- To what degree do the students achieve the expected learning outcomes?

	Before coaching cycle starts	Session 1	Session 2	Session 3	Session 4	Session 5	Follow-up
Level of support		TO "I do, you watch"	TO "I do, you watch"	WITH "I do, you help"	WITH "You do, I help"	BY "You do, I watch"	Based on teacher's need
Classroom time	Coach observes the teacher teach a lesson in the subject area and with the students who will be involved in coaching the cycle. Coach gathers as much information as possible about student and teacher strengths and needs and about what students are currently learning.	Coach demonstrates a lesson based on teacher's focus but without detailed co-planning with the teacher. Coach explicitly models the leverage point, or what coach and teacher determined will move the teacher's practice forward.	Coach demonstrates the co-planned lesson, using the teacher's ideas, words, and suggestions. Push pause to think aloud about teaching decisions. Explicitly model the leverage point.	Side-by-side, teach the co-planned lesson. Coach teaches "challenging parts" and teacher teaches "familiar parts." Push pause to discuss teaching decisions.	Side-by-side teach the co-planned lesson. Coach teaches "familiar parts" and teacher tries on "challenging parts."	Teacher teaches the bulk of the co-planned lesson with coach's support. Coach enters the lesson at the teacher's request or coach's discretion.	After the teacher has time to practice independently, the coach returns to provide support for the teacher based on teacher's needs.

Planning Time							
	Coach analyzes information about students and teacher to make decisions about the focus, or leverage point, of the coaching cycle. Coach meets with teacher to discuss the intent of the upcoming work and to get ideas about the content of Session 1's lesson.	Debrief lesson and co-plan Session 2 lesson. Be specific about the decisions you made during the lesson. Discuss the "teaching moves" made to support the students.	Debrief lesson and co-plan Session 3 lesson. Establish signals for entering and exiting the lesson. Determine roles—coach usually takes on "challenging parts" and teacher does "familiar parts."	Debrief lesson and co-plan Session 4 lesson. Evaluate side-by-side teaching. Determine roles—coach should emphasize planning for the "challenging parts" so that the teacher is prepared to do those parts.	Debrief lesson and co-plan Session 5 lesson. Evaluate gradual release. Establish support for Session 5—this is NOT going to be observation and feedback. Coach will be there to support the teacher at the teacher's request or at the coach's discretion.	Debrief coaching cycle. Plan for next steps.	Debrief the follow-up support and plan next steps.

Debriefs should always include discussion of the decisions made during the lesson to help the coach and teacher get clear about the decision-making processes each other is using.

Debriefs should always include discussion of evidence of student learning. What evidence do we have that students learned? What more do we need to do for their learning in the next lesson?

Co-planning should always involve paying attention to content (what students will know and be able to do) and pedagogy (how the teacher will support students in their learning). Co-planning should also include the coach supporting the teacher's content knowledge (what it means to teach reading and writing) and pedagogy (what students need for their learning).

FIG. 6–1 Possible five-session coaching cycle

What am I learning that could help shape the coaching focus?
- What are you, as coach, learning about the teacher and students that may become the focus of your coaching cycle?

Make sure to script everything so that you have information about the lesson to analyze.

Things to Consider About Your Coaching Focus and Method

Based on analysis of the lesson and conversations with the teacher, what does this teacher need next for her learning?

Which method of coaching makes sense?

What is possible given my schedule and the teacher's schedule?

Beginning a Gradual Release Coaching Cycle

If you decide that a gradual release coaching cycle is the method you are going to use, start preparing the lesson you will demonstrate during Session 1. Ask yourself:

What do you plan to demonstrate for the teacher?

How do you plan to gradually release responsibility to the teacher over the course of a few days?

Since you just did a classroom observation, you should have a sense of what the students are learning. Set aside time to meet with your teacher to discuss the process of a gradual release coaching cycle and to ask about what the students need next for their learning. Explain that you plan to start off the coaching cycle by demonstrating a lesson. Why? For a couple of reasons. First, since you just watched the teacher teach, it makes sense that the teacher should watch you teach. One of the most effective ways to build trust with a teacher is to actually show the teacher you know how to teach and that you are willing to stand in her shoes, enter the reality of her day-to-day teaching, and teach her students. Second, you won't expect a teacher to try anything that you haven't modeled. Third, you want to establish a relationship and rapport with her students so that you can get to know them as learners to help inform your instructional co-planning.

You need to know what the teacher has planned next for the students so that the lesson you demonstrate is aligned with the students' ongoing work. You could ask, "What is the focus for your next lesson? What do you expect students to know and be able to do as a result of your lesson? What materials were you planning to use?" You will use the teacher's focus and the teacher's materials to plan your lesson.

If the teacher plans to use a particular text, ask if you may use it. If the teacher uses ongoing charts, ask if you may add to the charts (I come prepared with sentence strips to add to the chart in case the teachers do not feel comfortable with me writing on their charts).

Planning the Lesson You Will Demonstrate

Make time to plan and prepare a well-crafted lesson. Remember that you are planning a lesson designed to teach students *and* a teacher. You need to plan with the student's needs and learning outcomes in mind: What do you want them to know and be able to do? How will you actually teach the lesson to meet their needs? And you need to consider the teacher's needs: What do you want the teacher to see you do? Don't forget to plan how you will model the teaching practices once you decide what your focus will be. What will you model explicitly? Prepare a "Look For" Sheet to help the teacher remember what to pay attention to as you demonstrate.

Plan places to think aloud as you teach so that you can explain to the teacher, in the moment, what you are doing and why. Students may give you strange looks the first time you talk to the teacher in the midst of your lesson, but they'll quickly grow accustomed to it.

You may also need to adjust the lesson focus the teacher gave you to create a lesson that honors the teacher's intent and also reflects your knowledge of best practice. This can be tricky. On the one hand, you want your lesson to fit into what students are studying and you want to show the teacher that you took into account her requests when you planned for the students, but on the other hand, if you do not agree with the focus of the lesson or do not believe the materials are appropriate for achieving the learning outcomes, you need to make adjustments so that you can demonstrate a lesson that meets student needs and reflects the type of teaching that will be the focus of your coaching cycle.

Why not just plan to demonstrate a lesson without involving the teacher's thinking? I used to do this all the time. I'd prepare a lesson based on my best thinking after a classroom observation, a lesson that I thought met student needs and that modeled the kind of teaching I wanted to work on with the teacher. But time and time again teachers said things like, "But that's not where we're going," or "That's not what my students need to learn." Because I neglected to involve them in the decision-making process, the lesson belonged to me, not to them, and the lesson I taught failed to model something within their zone of proximal development. Those lessons were significantly easier to plan, but off the mark.

Now I take the lesson focus and massage it into my lesson planning in a way that reflects my pedagogical content knowledge. I try my hardest to use the teacher's materials, modifying them if necessary and adding in materials of my own. For example, one teacher wanted me to do a seventh-grade reading lesson on identifying similes and metaphors using an overhead projector to display a sheet of statements, such as "Nobody invites Harold to parties because he is a wet blanket" and "The baby was like an octopus, grabbing at all the items on the grocery store shelves." The students were expected to read each statement and label it "simile" or "metaphor." I held onto the idea of similes and metaphors and crafted instead a reading lesson in which we read a story rich with figurative language, and discussed how the similes and metaphors helped us construct meaning. Another teacher wanted students to consider the historical context of a piece when analyzing a character's actions, words, thoughts, and behaviors, and gave me a short text about World War II, "In Response to Executive Order 9066" by Dwight Okita. But the students had not yet learned about Roosevelt ordering the internment of Japanese Americans following Pearl Harbor. I held onto both the focus and the text and added a second text, a brief expository description of the situation surrounding Executive Order 9066. I massaged the lesson into showing students how they can gain meaning from a text without knowing much about the historical context. And then I added on a portion, showing students how to enhance their meaning making by researching the historical context and then rereading a piece with this context in mind. In both examples I worked to honor the teacher's intent. I also made sure to use the first few minutes of the lesson to explain to the teachers how I used their ideas to shape my lesson and how I added my own thinking to the lesson, too.

Make sure you prepare a lesson plan for the lesson and make a copy for the teacher. If you plan to introduce a lesson-planning template, use it for planning the lessons you demonstrate so that your plan can serve as a model when you co-plan lessons.

Teaching the Session 1 Lesson

Take a few minutes at the beginning of your time in the classroom to have a chat with the teacher. Review what you intend to accomplish with the demonstration lesson. Briefly explain how you adapted and perhaps modified the teacher's plan. For example, "You'll notice how I took your idea of similes and metaphors and put it into a lesson that involves having the students read some poetry with me." Give the teacher the "Look For" Sheet and a copy of your lesson plan and any materials to help guide her observation of your work. Establish where the teacher will be as you teach—the closer to you and the students, the better. If you want the teacher to participate in the lesson, for example, by listening in to partnerships alongside you, let her know your expectations.

Remind the students that you and the teacher are partners in your work together and that you appreciate their patience when you pause the lesson from time to time to talk to the teacher.

Keep track of your pacing! If you go on too much longer than the teacher can devote to a daily lesson, the teacher may become frustrated and dismiss your lesson. A common refrain heard when a demonstration runs long is, "If I had that kind of time, I would be able to do that type of teaching, too." I actually teach with a digital timer because I tend to lose track of time. I set the timer to go off five minutes before the end of my lesson to remind me to start closing the lesson. I also glance at it throughout the lesson to pace the lesson.

Debriefing and Planning Session 2

The purpose of the debrief after demonstrating a lesson in a gradual release coaching cycle is to use the lesson to start a conversation about upcoming work. Often debriefs of lessons focus too much on how to improve the lesson that just happened. It is only is helpful to analyze lessons and strategize how to make better instructional decisions if you plan to apply the insights to future teaching situations. If you plan to reteach the same lesson, fine-tuning that lesson is appropriate and useful. If the lesson is over and is probably not going to be retaught by either of you, it is more useful to apply what you both learned from the lesson to the planning of your next lesson than to refine the lesson you just taught.

Here's how you can discuss your demonstration in a manner that helps you plan the next steps:

◆ What did you observe about the students that can help us think about tomorrow's lesson?

◆ I asked you to look for _____. What did you notice? What questions do you have about _____?

◆ What did I do to support the students that you think we should include in our planning?

- What more could I have done to support the students that we should include in our planning?

- What did you see me do that you would like to try?

These questions certainly allow analysis and critique of the lesson and do so in a way that allows whatever you both learned from the experience to be applied to the next lesson. Take notes so that you can capture ideas for your work together.

Be sure to allow time for your teacher to pick your brain about the decisions you made during your lesson. You may be asked questions like, "Do you always . . . ?" or "Do you ever . . . ?" or "What would you do if . . . ?" The advantage of working together for consecutive days is that you do not have to give a detailed response during the debrief. The teaching you do together will probably answer many of the initial debrief questions, so rather than explain an idea you anticipate will arise in the upcoming days, take note of the questions so that you can revisit them throughout the coaching cycle. You can respond with statements like, "We have a few days together, so we'll get to see if I always or ever do certain things."

You probably will not have enough time to plan the lesson in detail and that is deliberate, for two reasons: first it is more important for the teacher to be able to discuss the lesson you just demonstrated, your teaching moves, and your upcoming coaching work together than for you to rush right into planning the next lesson; second, because repetition is a key ingredient to success, you will want your teacher to see you model another lesson before having to create a detailed lesson plan with you. Reserve time to explicitly discuss the plan for Session 2, taking note of what the teacher thinks the students should know and be able to do as a lesson, her ideas about how you might teach the students, and her requests for what she hopes to see you do.

Notice how your lesson planning is following a gradual release of responsibility model, too. You planned the first lesson you demonstrated using the teacher's focus and materials, to provide a model of how you plan. For the second lesson, you are adding more of the teacher's ideas to the plan, but you are still planning the lesson to provide a second model. For the third and fourth lessons, you and the teacher make decisions together and co-plan the lessons, shifting from your planning the challenging parts to the teacher's planning the challenging parts. For the fifth lesson, the teacher takes on the bulk of the responsibility for planning all of the parts of the lesson, with your assistance when needed.

Teaching the Session 2 Lesson

Spend a few minutes talking with the teacher before you start demonstrating your lesson, again providing a copy of your lesson plan and a new "Look For" Sheet. Explain any last-minute decisions you've made about the lesson and remind the teacher that in the debrief, the two of you will plan how you are going to share the responsibility of teaching the Session 3 lesson. Figure out where the teacher is going to be during the lesson. As you teach, remember to push pause and think aloud, making explicit your teaching decisions.

Debriefing and Planning Session 3

Debrief the lesson, emphasizing what happened during the first two sessions to help inform decision making for Session 3. Because you now have taught two consecutive lessons, you can start to compare and contrast the decisions you made during both, and judge how those decisions affected the students. Some of the "do you ever or do you always" questions are already answered, and other questions will arise. Remember to explain your thinking whenever you make statements. Even if your reasoning seems obvious and unnecessary to share, err of the side of explaining yourself. For example, if you moved students around in the middle of the lesson, explain why or ask, "Did you notice I moved a few students around? Do you know why I did that?" Or, if you decided to call on certain children and not others, again, explain why. Remember that you are striving to make the invisible visible. You can always ask, "Are my explanations helpful?"

Co-planning Session 3 may be stressful for both the teacher and you; for the teacher because she now needs to do parts of the lesson, and for you because you are wondering if you are releasing responsibility too soon or not soon enough; you want the teacher to be successful; and you need to think about the students, the teacher, and yourself as you teach, and that is a lot to think about and manage. Plus, side-by-side teaching may be new to both of you, and because by definition you cannot become good at it alone, the two of you will be learning to side-by-side teach together.

Use the two lessons you demonstrated to guide how you will side-by-side teach. Talk about what happened in both lessons, what the teacher feels comfortable trying (the familiar parts), and what she wants to see you demonstrate a third time (the challenging parts). If the teacher wants to see you do the entire lesson again, remind her that you are gradually releasing responsibility of the lesson and that you'll be there, right by her side, as she tries her new learning. Remember to talk about your signals for entering the lesson—how you will enter the lesson and how your teacher will request your help—and how you will hand the lesson back to the teacher. Be as specific as you can with your lesson planning, knowing that you will adjust it as you teach together and respond to both the students' and teacher's needs.

Side-by-Side Teaching the Session 3 Lesson

You are now at the point where you are gradually releasing responsibility of part of the teaching to the teacher, which means the teacher will be trying on new learning and probably feeling quite unsteady. Before you begin, spend a few extra minutes talking with the teacher. Review the plan, check for understanding about who will do what, adjust the teaching space to make sure both of you can fit next to each other, and remind the teacher to try to pay attention to your parts, since she will try on those parts tomorrow. The teacher may want to explain to the students how the teaching is going to look. Be flexible as you teach together because lessons rarely go exactly as planned. Be prepared for the teacher to get pretty flustered by the process and ask you to finish the lesson. Side-by-side teaching the first time is unnerving for the teacher because there is so much to think about—not only is she trying on new learning, she is doing it with you by her side (which is supportive, but also unusual). Be as clear as you can when you hand back the lesson.

Debriefing and Planning Session 4

Celebrate any successes you both achieved during the side-by-side lesson! Again, use what you learned to help you plan the next lesson. Talk about what worked and what needs revision. You are aiming to release more of the responsibility to the teacher, provided she is ready. In Session 3 you most likely modeled the challenging parts while the teacher taught the more familiar parts. In Session 4, try to release to the teacher the responsibility of tackling the challenge. You will still be providing support by whispering in and by teaching the more familiar parts of the lesson. Teachers often wonder why, if they already did the familiar parts successfully, they shouldn't just teach the whole lesson. The reason you will still teach part of the lesson is to give the teacher time during the lesson to prepare to take on the challenging parts. Create a detailed plan now, with learning outcomes for the students and an outline of your roles during the lesson.

Side-by-Side Teaching the Session 4 Lesson

Start with a quick conversation with the teacher, focusing your talk on her role, and reminding her that you are ready to provide your support if she needs it. Teaching side-by-side should feel a bit more comfortable. Monitor yourself vigilantly because when the teacher starts to struggle a bit or veers from the plan, you may want to jump in and get the lesson back on course. The point of teaching side-by-side is to be responsive to the teacher's needs, not to make sure the lesson goes according to plan.

For example, I side-by-side taught with a teacher, Joshua, whose biggest challenge was remembering to probe for thinking after a student responded. He tended to probe only when students were mistaken, which meant the class tended to hear only erroneous thinking. We worked on using prompts like, "What made you say that?" and "What led you to that idea?" whenever a student offered an idea, and on how to listen to student responses. During Session 4, we planned that Joshua would do the bulk of the teaching—read the text, model his thinking, get students talking about ideas in the text, and, most important, remember to probe for thinking—and that I would then use the student responses to move the students' ideas toward a conversation. As we taught, I noticed that Joshua started asking student after student to share her or his thinking. One after the next, Joshua probed for thinking, then turned to me and said, "This is awesome! I know we're supposed to keep going in this lesson, but hearing the students' thinking is fascinating!" Rather than sticking to our plan, I whispered to him to read more of the text so that the students had more to talk about and, rather than shifting into conversation, to keep asking students to share ideas and their thinking. Joshua was experiencing success and the students were responding intelligently. Moving the students toward growing a conversation together could wait so that Joshua could savor his success.

Debriefing and Planning Session 5

After celebrating your successes, start talking about how you envision the next lesson. What do students need next? What does the teacher need next? Presuming this is the last lesson you may do together for a while, it is important that the teacher experience success managing the bulk of the lesson. You want the teacher to feel confident in her ability to apply her new learning to her work when you are no longer side-by-side. Spend time carefully designing the lesson so that the teacher has a clear plan for support. Talk about what level of support the teacher wants from you, from mostly observing and giving feedback at the end of the lesson, to sitting in her line of vision, nodding encouragingly, to you sitting by her side, ready to assist when necessary. And explain that you expect to assist because the learning is still relatively new. Some teachers like the coach to fill out a "Look For" Sheet to get feedback on specific aspects of the lesson.

Supporting the Teaching of the Session 5 Lesson

As before, talk with the teacher before the start of the lesson, reviewing the plan, answering any lingering questions, and establishing where you will be physically during the lesson. Ask the teacher whether she anticipates any places where she expects to call on you for assistance, or whether she prepared a "Look For" Sheet. Be as encouraging and supportive as you can. People describe me as having a "serious thinking face," and occasionally teachers I coach tell me they think my expression means they are doing something wrong as they teach. I have to remind myself to smile and nod, especially during Session 5, because the teacher is extra sensitive to visual and physical responses. Be prepared to whisper in, but only if the teacher requests support. Whenever I watch teachers teach on the day I've released most of the responsibility to them, I actually count to ten mentally each time I think I should jump into the lesson to help. That gives the teacher time to fumble and recover while I calm my overly eager tendencies to help.

Debriefing and Planning Next Steps

During the debrief, applaud the growth and new learning you, the teacher, and the students experienced together. Ask the teacher to talk about what she learned from the gradual release coaching experience and what she intends to continue to practice in the upcoming days. And ask the teacher what she learned about her students during the week and how that information will help inform her planning. Take time to specifically name and celebrate the growth you've seen during the week. We all enjoy hearing about our successes. Reiterate any specific teaching moves that you want the teacher to continue to practice, and jot them down in your notes for your record keeping and follow-up.

Allow time to plan lessons for the upcoming week. After such intense planning support, it can be a big adjustment for the teacher to go back to planning in isolation. If you brainstorm lessons together for the next week, the teacher will more likely continue to practice her new skills.

Get your calendar out and schedule a follow-up visit in a week or two. The follow-up visit serves several purposes: first, it gives you an opportunity to provide continued support; second, it serves as a reminder that you expect to see the outcome of the lessons you co-planned; third, it motivates the teacher to continue to practice her new learning.

 ## Unit of Study Coaching Cycle

Another way to consider organizing your coaching work is to do so within a unit of study to help teachers learn how to support student learning over several weeks. Since many teachers organize their teaching into studies—often described as units of study, genre studies, units of inquiry, or theme studies—it makes sense to coach teachers throughout a unit (Calkins 2003). We know that as the unit progresses, the types of lessons we teach and the teaching decisions we make shift to support the students' growing understanding of the concepts and processes we are teaching. Teachers and students can benefit from a coach's support at various times throughout the unit to help answer questions that may arise, such as:

- What do the lessons look like at the beginning, during the middle, and toward the end of a unit of study?

- What do I do if students aren't "getting it"?

- How do I provide support both for those who struggle and those who move along quickly?

- How do I teach lessons from the various steps in the writing process (immersion, collection, choosing an idea, crafting, drafting, revising, getting ready to publish)?

You cannot help teachers answer these questions if you only concentrate your work within a gradual release coaching cycle. You can if you spread out your time with teachers and schedule ample time to help describe and plan the lessons that teachers can use between your visits.

Coaching within a unit of study also helps you support an entire grade or department level at the same time if you select a unit that all participating teachers agree to try on. And it helps provide a grade level of students with a relatively consistent educational experience that future teachers can build upon. Of course, freeing up teachers to observe and participate in the work will require conversations with your principal and artful manipulation of teachers' schedules. Here's how it looks to organize coaching within a unit of study.

Determine Which Unit Will Be the Focus of Your Coaching Work and How Long the Unit Is Expected to Last

You may be coaching in a school that has mapped out a curriculum calendar to help teachers manage their time effectively throughout the year. If so, determine which unit will be the focus of your coaching work. If not, as a grade level or department decide on a unit that everyone agrees to teach. Determine how long the study is expected to last and then add two weeks to your coaching schedule—a week prior to the start of the unit to preplan, gather materials, and set the stage for the coaching work and a week after the end of the unit to examine student work to determine the unit's effectiveness, to make any changes, and to help prepare teachers for the next unit.

Determine Who Will Be Your Lead Teacher for the Unit and Who Will Be the Observing Teachers

By working in one classroom throughout the unit, you can provide ongoing coaching support for a teacher and see how the work is affecting a group of students. Since teaching is about being responsive to student needs, it is essential that you work with the same group of students throughout the unit. Determine who will be your lead teacher for the unit, knowing that when you coach within another unit with the same grade level or department, one of the observing teachers will become the lead teacher.

Establish your expectations for how the work will progress. The lead teacher has the most intense responsibility because the demonstrations and coaching work are happening in her classroom with her students and, accordingly, she gets your direct coaching support. The observing teachers are expected to try on the lessons that you, as a team, co-planned and discussed, and that they observed (modified to meet their students' needs, of course). Observing teachers are expected to share their own experiences of trying on the lessons and to bring samples of student work, co-constructed charts, and useful resources and materials to analyze together and share with the group. The goal is for everyone involved to benefit by directly applying the learning from the unit of study coaching work in their own classrooms, and then using their classroom experiences to inform continuing coaching work. If only the coach and lead teacher try on the work, students and teachers across the grade level will not benefit.

Schedule Your Time Together

Spread your coaching days across the unit. If you have eight coaching sessions to spread across a four-week unit, for example, schedule one for the week prior to when you plan to start the unit and one for the week after you plan to end the unit. Then schedule the remaining six sessions based on when it makes sense according to the lead teacher's strengths and needs, when observing teachers can be freed up to attend, and when your schedule allows.

If your schedule permits only once a week on Mondays, work within that constraint. If you can add an additional session or two, add it, based on when you anticipate the teacher may need additional support. For example, when I coached a teacher through the writing process, I anticipated that drafting and revising might be challenging because the teacher revealed that her students just wanted to copy over what they had written, make a few cosmetic changes, and be done. I scheduled two sessions in her class that week, one focused on drafting and, two days later, the other focused on revision. When you can schedule your coaching work to correspond with times the teacher anticipates needing your support, you are better poised for success.

Schedule time for the actual work in the classroom as well as time to meet with the group to debrief the lesson and discuss and plan lessons that should happen before the next scheduled coaching session. By lesson planning as a group, you build capacity among the teachers because they have ownership in the process, can share resources, and can problem-solve anticipated issues. Remind participating teachers that though they are trying to keep pace with each other so that they can learn from each other's experiences, they may need to adjust their pacing to meet their students' needs.

Create the Expectation That Teachers Are Responsible for Trying on Strategies Learned Through Classroom Coaching

A gradual release coaching cycle and unit of study coaching cycle provide teachers with high levels of support, and involve a great deal of time, energy, and commitment from both teachers and coach. With high levels of support come high expectations. Coaches and teachers should collaboratively establish goals and expectations before, during, and after the coaching cycle. These are not supervisory expectations, but the expectations of colleagues who have just spent an intense amount of effort to make instructional changes, set so that all of their work won't be for naught.

We are each responsible for holding ourselves to high levels of professional conduct and continued professional growth and improvement. As a coach, I strive to better my coaching work every day just as I strove to improve my teaching as a classroom teacher. People may describe me as self-motivated and disciplined. In reality, I am also an overextended, multitasking procrastinator who needs firm deadlines and accountability to drive me to actually accomplish the many goals I set for myself. Similarly, the teachers with whom I work have myriad responsibilities and need time lines and clear expectations in order to implement changes in their classroom practice.

Be clear about the time line for the work. How soon should the teacher be incorporating the techniques you have worked on together? What needs to happen between coaching sessions so that the students and teacher are prepared for the next lessons? What is the time line for moving from demonstrating to side-by-side coaching to the teacher taking on most of the work? What needs to be gathered by the teacher or by you for the next meeting? Clarity and deadlines are required if busy professionals are to stay on track. When you build a productive and trusting relationship with a teacher, both of you should expect high levels of accountability to your work. I often use email (Figure 6–2) as a way to remind teachers of our mutual expectations.

Problem-Solving When Your Coaching Work Does Not Take Hold

Yes, high levels of support imply high expectations, and of course, you want to see that your coaching work is taking hold. But what happens if you visit a classroom after a gradual release or unit of study coaching cycle and you don't see what you expect to see? First of all, *don't* go to the principal with your concerns. If you have concerns about a teacher's practice, your responsibility is to first raise those concerns with the teacher, not the principal. Reflect on the quality of your coaching. Is the teacher mimicking your teaching practices? Could what you have identified as a concern simply be a misunderstanding of an idea raised in your coaching conversations? Be ready to provide the teacher with supports for addressing those concerns.

I coached Gabriella, a seventh-grade language arts teacher in a school working on providing students with more cognitively demanding learning experiences. I demonstrated two reading lessons, co-planned a third lesson,

Monday, after school
To: Jonathan
From: Katherine
Re: Upcoming work

Hi Jonathan,

Wow! Don't you feel great about how quickly you've moved your students away from writing about topics they think you want them to write about to topics that truly interest them? As we conferred with students today, I hope you heard how excited Trevor and Ja'shanee are about investigating why the public libraries had to drastically reduce Sunday hours. On her way out of class, Ja'shanee asked me if she will be able to send her persuasive essay to the City Council or to the newspaper when she's done. She's fired up!

Here's a reminder of what we agreed to do between now and next Monday when I'll be in your room again. We planned the minilessons on helping students gather information, how to craft and conduct interviews, becoming aware of the counterarguments, and writing a "call to action." We have four minilessons for five days because you know my rule of thumb—if it is the first time you're trying the lesson, plan that it will take a bit longer than you expected. Try to be aware of your pacing without getting frustrated.

I will be looking for more exemplars of persuasive essays today and tomorrow. I'll make sure that I have those in your mailbox by Wednesday morning so that you can continue to add to the mentor text box.

On Monday we're going to co-teach the lesson, even though I know you'd rather I demonstrate ☺. You've already taken the class through two writing cycles so drafting isn't new to you. But I know you're nervous about modeling how to gather all of the persuasive essay ideas into a draft, so we'll teach it together. Let me know if the planning meeting we set up during lunch on Monday still works for you. If not, we'll need to meet to plan on Friday so we're ready.

Your students are ready for the persuasive essay lessons and are excited, thanks to your teaching. Email me if you have any questions, OK?

FIG. 6–2 Expectations reminder

and we decided to side-by-side teach the third lesson together. In our planning we spent time crafting higher-level thinking questions based on Bloom's taxonomy and planned how we would model using think-aloud. Our side-by-side teaching went well, Gabriella was excited about her successful use of higher-level questions, and we eagerly co-planned her fourth lesson. A few days later I dropped by for a follow-up visit and was dismayed to find Gabriella asking literal questions. Did I not coach well enough? Was the teacher deciding not to take on the work? What was going on?

The principal and I met that same day for our weekly check-in meeting and she asked me about my coaching work with Gabriella. I only shared our co-planning and side-by-side successes, not my concerns, since I had not yet had a chance to speak with Gabriella. At the end of the day, Gabriella asked me what I thought of her lesson, and I replied, "I noticed you were asking lots of questions, and many were at the literal level. What was your experience of the lesson?" She responded, "I'm so glad you said that! I thought I had higher-level questioning down pat in my teaching, but the students just stare at me when I ask them hard questions. When you and I were teaching together that didn't happen. I'm really frustrated by my lack of progress and I am slipping back into asking them literal questions, which they can answer."

I reminded Gabriella that not only did we ask higher-level questions, we modeled how to answer those questions using think-alouds. Gabriella immediately realized that she wasn't modeling enough and said she would try to in tomorrow's lesson. If that lesson didn't go well, she said, she would need more support from me in planning questioning and modeling. Thank goodness I went to Gabriella with my concerns instead of to the principal! I could have damaged our relationship based on my ignorance, not on her lack of willingness to hold herself responsible for improving her practice.

Not all my coaching relationships are as strong as the one Gabriella and I built together. From time to time, despite everything I know how to do to build a productive relationship, I feel as though I am wasting my time because the teacher is not taking on the work. When this happens, I am up front with the teacher about my frustration, have conversations, and, if that doesn't work, recommend that we schedule a triad meeting with the principal to address my concerns (Figure 6–3). When a teacher suspects that the coach is having discussions with the principal about her practice behind her back, the coaching relationship becomes toxic. So, rather than meeting with the principal before the triad meeting to discuss my concerns, I wait until the triad meeting so that we are all in the same room—teacher, principal, and

11/05
To: Rebecca (principal) and Sue (sixth-grade teacher)
From: Katherine (school-based coach)
Re: Triad meeting

Hi Rebecca and Sue,

I am emailing you both a request to set up a triad meeting as early next week as possible. As you and I have discussed, Sue, I believe the three of us need an opportunity to redefine our coaching relationship and to problem-solve the obstacles in our way.

Rebecca and Sue, once you find a date/time in common, I'll make adjustments to my schedule to make sure we can have our triad meeting. Thank you in advance for arranging the triad meeting.

FIG. 6–3 Triad meeting email

literacy coach—and together can problem-solve the coaching relationship. Usually the triad meetings result in a mutually satisfying resolution, sometimes making us both aware of some shortcomings in our coaching relationship that we can remedy and, occasionally, others that we cannot. Even when we decide to discontinue our coaching cycle work, we continue to work together in other professional development structures.

Coaching Cycles Within the Bigger Context of Your Work

Are you intrigued by the coaching cycle concept? Trying to fit one into your schedule? Thinking about with whom you might give it a try? Not sure you or your teachers (or both) are up for the intensity yet? You'll know if the time is right. You'll find yourself saying, "I wish I could just get into my teachers' classrooms and help them out for a few days" or you'll hear your teachers expressing the same sentiment. When I start working with teachers, I don't use coaching cycles. Teachers first need many opportunities to observe lessons and get some less intense experiences under their belts. That's why this chapter follows the discussion in Chapter 5 of the eight ways of studying instruction. Coaching cycles are more successful after teachers have built a vision with you for the type of instruction you'll be working on together. And coaching cycles should come after you've had ample opportunity to develop your coaching skills. When you're ready for your first gradual release coaching cycle, find a friendly teacher who will give you a soft place to land when you fumble in your coaching work, a teacher who delights in the hard work of figuring out teaching and learning, a teacher with whom you will likely enjoy an unforgettable learning experience.

Professional Development Workshops and Sessions

After examining intensive coaching cycles where the focus is on providing individual teachers with support at their points of need, the next step is to expand the scale to give large groups of teachers intense levels of support at the same time. Since many schools utilize whole-staff sessions as one of their primary methods of professional development, the likelihood is great that you play a large role in designing and facilitating those sessions. Your responsibilities probably include helping determine the focus, creating an engaging session, attending to the organizational details, leading or co-leading the session, being prepared to support teachers in their classrooms after the session, following up on the effect of the session on teaching and learning, and then beginning the process anew. Your sessions may have a variety of configurations—whole staff, small group by department, grade level, or common need—depending on who needs the learning and on how people learn best. Since much of the work I do happens in workshops, I've had to figure out ways to engage large groups of educators in rich, value-adding experiences.

The guiding principles described in this chapter apply not just to workshops, but to any situation where adults come together to learn. They are relevant here because whole-staff or large-group workshops require us to be particularly aware of the experiences we provide teachers so that we can affect instructional practice.

Many people belittle whole-staff workshops as light-impact time-wasters. I disagree. When we provide experiences that are immediately applicable to teaching situations, it makes a difference for teachers. We cannot fully replicate every teacher's classroom environment, but we can bring students to the session, either live or on video or through their data and student work. We cannot stand side-by-side with every teacher, problem-solving and making decisions in the moment, but we can create experiences that require and nurture the spirit of collaborative decision making. We can incorporate the ways of looking at instruction described in the past two chapters to bring teaching and learning alive. Carefully designed sessions that contain specific and well-crafted experiences can be a major tool for changing teachers' knowledge and skill.

 ## Pay Attention to the Details

Before exploring the principles of adult learning, let's address the organizational aspects. After leading a series of workshops for hundreds of teachers one summer, my coach colleagues and I reviewed the exit slips from the sessions—which ranged from half-day to full-day to weeklong—to identify patterns and trends across all our workshops. Initially we chuckled when we read comments like, "thanks for the snacks in the afternoon," "the mid-morning break was energizing," "setting up the room to mimic a classroom gave me so many ideas," and "thanks for bringing in regular lamps instead of using the overhead fluorescent lights." Nearly all the exit slips contained some feedback on what we did to help participants stay focused. Weeks of planning and thoughtful crafting of our sessions and participants were impressed with snacks, breaks, and room arrangement and environment. We got the message: the details matter.

Here's a list of details to consider when you're planning professional development sessions:

◆ **Room arrangement**—How you arrange a room reflects your beliefs about learning environments and affects the learning that occurs, so be thoughtful about how you want learning to occur. I try to set up my workshop space as I would a classroom, with a meeting area for discussions and tables for groups of four to six for collaborative work. How many people do you want sitting together for small-group work? Can participants see each other's faces during whole-group discussions? Is there space to set up materials for easy distribution and access? When you bring in a group of students for a demonstration lesson, where can you situate the lesson so that teachers can see and hear you and the students?

If you gather as a whole staff in the same location each time and you can leave up the charts and other evidence of your work, the reminders of

FIG. 7–1 Professional development room

previous work help build continuity. When you meet for workshops in smaller groups, consider holding the sessions in different teachers' classrooms, with permission of course, so that colleagues have opportunities to experience learning in each other's classroom environments. Have the hosting teacher give a five-minute "tour" before you start.

◆ **Seating arrangement**—Growing up, my family attended church together and always sat on the left side, three-quarters of the way up to the front. Other families staked out their locations, too, creating a predictable seating arrangement that was disrupted only by visitors who inadvertently sat in "someone else's" pew. I thought this self-assigned seating arrangement was unique to church until I noticed the same phenomenon in the school cafeteria and, later, in my college classes and in teacher workshops. People like to sit where they like to sit, and professional development sessions are no exception.

Sometimes it may not matter who sits with whom and where, and other times it may, depending on what and how you want teachers to learn. Like a teacher working with students in a classroom, decide how you want participants to sit: By grade level or department? in mixed grade-level or department teams? each new teacher paired with an experienced teacher? When you do assign seats, make finding them easy for teachers. I like to number the tables and then put teachers' table numbers next to their names on the sign-in sheet. Or I may draw a quick schematic on the board or overhead. Someone invariably groans about having assigned seats, which is why I always provide a rationale for my seating decisions, often prior to the session in my reminder email (see Figure 7–2).

◆ **Breaks**—Be considerate of your teachers' needs and schedule time for breaks if you meet for longer than ninety minutes.

◆ **Drinks and snacks**—Providing bottles of water and something to nibble on throughout the session goes a long way to setting up an environment conducive to adult learning.

To: Whole Staff
From: Katherine
Re: Tomorrow's professional development session

Hi everyone,

Just a quick note to remind you that we are meeting in the library tomorrow at 2:30 to continue our work on writing about reading.

Last time we met, we agreed that this session we'll bring samples of student responses to a whole-class read-aloud (pre-K and K teachers, you said you'll bring your chart pads with your class' co-constructed responses).

We're going to start the session sitting by grade level to give you a chance to examine the work of other students at the same grade level. After the break, we're going to sit in cross-grade-level groups so that we can begin to look at the progression of student responses as they move up the grades.

By the way, tomorrow's agenda is posted next to the mailboxes in the office. I'm really looking forward to our work together.

FIG. 7–2 Professional development session reminder

◆ **Time**—Be mindful of time. Unless there are extenuating circumstances, start on time, whether or not everyone is present. When you develop a reputation as someone who starts on time, participants are more likely to arrive on time, and those who rush to be there on time will appreciate that you respect their promptness. Strive to end on time (or even a few minutes early) and take breaks when scheduled, too. If you go long, people lose their focus on the work and start to worry more about missing the break or being late for whatever they have scheduled after the session.

◆ **Agenda**—Prepare and distribute an agenda for the session as soon as you have it ready, even though it may shift during the session. Knowing what to expect during a session helps teachers gear up for the learning. Often I email or post the agenda in a public space like the office or on the door of the meeting location the day before or morning of the session.

◆ **An overhead projector, document cameras, computer projectors, and whiteboards**—I get so frustrated when I cannot see what a presenter is showing us during a workshop. Be sure your equipment is in good working order before the session begins. Plug in equipment, position it so everyone can see the images, and clean it up if you need to. My colleagues tease me about my freezer bags of dry-erase board wipes and glass cleaner wipes until they need to borrow my supply to clean up a dirty whiteboard or overhead projector. Use a font size of at least 20 when making overheads so that they can be read. When showing a video, make sure the tape is cued and the volume is adjusted. And go easy on the zoom feature of a document camera, lest your participants get seasick.

◆ **Power strips**—With the increased use of laptop computers comes the increased need for access to an outlet. If your teachers tend to bring their computers to professional development sessions, consider purchasing power strips with long extension cords so that teachers don't have to vie for or sit around the perimeter of the room near the only available outlets.

◆ **Display space**—Determine where you want to display co-constructed charts, recommended texts, the workshop agenda, or any other visuals. Displaying materials from previous sessions serves as a reminder of past work and helps build continuity between and among sessions.

◆ **"Parking Lot" for ongoing communication**—In addition to asking participants to voice questions, concerns, or suggestions, develop a method for gathering in writing participants' questions, concerns, or suggestions throughout sessions. I either hang up a blue pocket chart and encourage participants to jot down their ideas on index cards or I hang up chart paper and

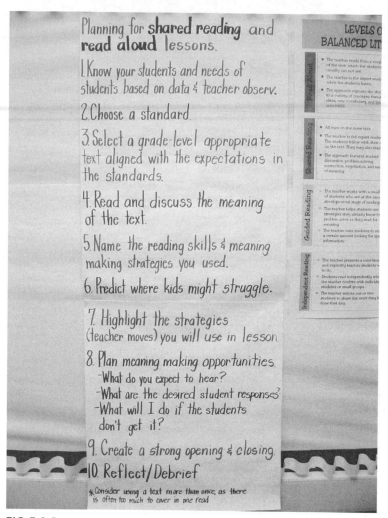

FIG. 7–3 Reminder of a past professional development session

encourage participants to use stickies. Often I jot down questions or issues that I know we cannot address during the session and "park" them on the chart paper or in the blue pocket chart as visual reminders of what we need to address in future sessions.

◆ **Supplies**—Because teachers usually rush to workshops, anticipate that they may forget to bring everything they need. I keep a supply of pens, pencils, sticky notes, three-by-five-inch index cards, and markers for charting in containers I put on each table during workshops.

164

◆ **Sources**—Teachers appreciate knowing the websites, Internet paths, and titles and authors of materials. Remember to indicate in writing the sources of the materials you use and distribute them during workshops so that teachers can access the source after the session. When I create handouts on my computer, I try to remember to put information in the footer that reminds teachers when and where they received the handout.

◆ **Multiple copies of handouts**—Some teachers are reluctant to write on handouts such as planning templates or texts during workshops because they want to have a clean copy to photocopy for their own use. Either encourage participants to write on stickies or give them each two copies.

Guiding Principles of Designing Adult Learning Within Professional Development Sessions

After dealing with the organizational and environment details, focus on crafting the content of the session. When I plan professional development sessions, I use the same decision-making cycle that I use to plan for students. In graduate school, the cycle we used read, "Plan, Teach, Reflect, Apply." Maybe because I tend to be literal when I learn something new, or maybe because it is a stage beginning teachers move through, I spent a great deal of time planning lessons, teaching lessons, and reflecting on those lessons. My teaching work continued in this fashion until I realized, with the help of my coaches and principal, that teaching isn't about teaching *lessons*. Teaching is about teaching *students*. Effective lessons aren't those that go according to plan. Effective lessons are lessons that are based on student needs, respond to student needs in the midst of their learning, and result in students' learning what they needed next.

Here are four principles to keep in mind:

1. The Decision-Making Cycle for Effective Instruction (Figure 7–4). As literacy coaches, we juggle both what students need next for their learning, since our work is about improving student achievement through the improvement of instruction, and what teachers need next for their learning. Just as effective lessons are ones that result in student achievement, effective professional development sessions are ones that result in increased teacher knowledge and skill that results in increased student achievement. I revised the decision-making cycle I learned in graduate

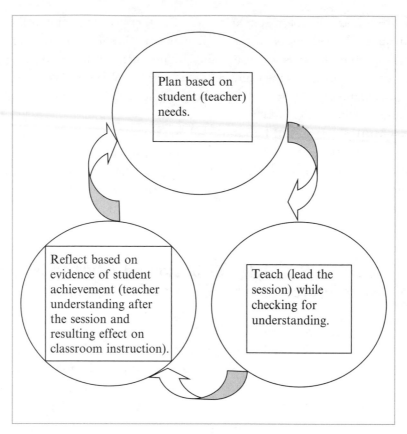

FIG. 7–4 Decision-making cycle for effective instruction

school to include reminders that coaching focuses on students, teachers, and lessons.

2. Vygotsky's Zone of Proximal Development. Just as students thrive when instruction is aimed within their zone of proximal development, so do adults. What can your teachers already do? What can your teachers almost do? Based on what your teachers have been working on and what your schoolwide focus is, what makes sense to do next? If you choose to work on something too far outside their zone of proximal development, teachers are likely to become frustrated. The delicate dance of choosing the right focus for a whole group of teachers during professional development is the same dance teachers perform as they design lessons.

3. Cambourne's Conditions of Learning. Brian Cambourne's (1988) conditions of learning—immersion, demonstration, engagement, expectation, use, approximation, and response—need to be present for students to progress as readers, and for adults to progress as educators.

4. Gradual Release of Responsibility. Just as students benefit from instruction that follows the gradual release of responsibility—to, with, and by— so, too, do adults (Pearson and Gallagher 1983).

When I plan professional development sessions, I keep in mind the decision-making cycle for effective instruction, Vygotsky's zone of proximal development, Cambourne's conditions of learning, and Pearson and Gallagher's gradual release of responsibility. The more experience you gain designing, implementing, and reflecting on professional development sessions, the better you'll become at using these theories in your planning.

 ## Keep the Learning Real

As I plan for adult learning, keeping in mind authentic learning experiences in which I gained knowledge and skill helps me remember to pay attention to how people learn. Take a moment to remember a time when you learned a new skill. Under what conditions did you learn best? What kind of support did you receive? What worked for you? What did not work for you?

When I turned sixteen, I started taking driver's education classes. As one of the youngest people in my junior class, I was eager to get my license, since everyone else seemed to be driving already. My parents enrolled me in a driver's education class, where we learned the basics of how a car works, studied the rules of the road, learned to change a tire, and watched videos of accidents to deter drunk driving. The instructor expected us to memorize the information and to be ready to describe what we should do in various driving scenarios. We also had time behind the wheel of a car, with a saintly driving instructor sitting on the passenger side, which was equipped with a brake and steering wheel. Sessions with the driving instructor went well as we progressed from driving in an empty parking lot to a deserted series of back roads, to busier streets, to the highway. Though I could remember the rules of the road and the basic mechanics of operating a vehicle, coordinating my knowledge and skill took practice, confidence, and assistance. Each session involved trial and error, lots of verbal instruction, and an occasional wresting of control by the instructor. I vividly remember having to switch lanes on the highway and panicking midway into the left lane. Fortunately, the instructor took control and guided me off the highway. Accident avoided. Moments later he guided me back onto the highway, knowing that if he did not, I may be too frightened to try again. With successes, my confidence soared, my skills improved, and I earned my license.

So what did I need for my learning? I needed all of Cambourne's conditions to be present: *immersion* in the nuts and bolts of driving knowledge; repeated *demonstrations* of every aspect of driving; the *expectation* that I could gain the necessary knowledge, skill, experience, and confidence to drive in a variety of conditions; *engagement* in first discussing various driving scenarios and then actually getting behind the wheel and trying everything myself; supervised *practice or use* for six months, beginning with a teacher who expected *approximation* and had a brake and a steering wheel to help guide me, and moving to my parents, who wished they had similar controls; *responsibility* in operating the vehicle; continual *feedback and response* that ranged from continual explanation of what to do and how to do it, to stern warnings, to encouragement and praise. I needed my instructor to be acutely aware of what was within my *zone of proximal development*. Too far out of my zone could be dangerous, because I either could become complacent about driving if the tasks were too simple or could cause harm if the tasks were too challenging. Thank goodness my instructor didn't expect me to watch him drive and then just drive on my own. I needed him to gradually release responsibility to me over time and in increasingly complex driving conditions while remaining ready to take over when I needed more support.

The purpose of driver's ed is to graduate students who have the knowledge and skill they need to drive safely. Similarly, the purpose of professional development sessions is to improve teacher knowledge and *skill* so that classroom instruction and learning is affected. But too often I attend professional development that errs on the side of emphasizing knowledge over skill. We discuss professional texts, analyze student work, develop rubrics, watch instructional videos, read and discuss children's literature, create curriculum maps, and share classroom experiences, and leave feeling smarter about learning and teaching. But we stop short of actually discussing and figuring out how to turn the new knowledge into instructional skill.

If we don't work on developing our instructional skills, we are left with unanswered questions such as, How do I use the ideas in the professional texts in my own classroom tomorrow? Can someone show me? What does a more effective lesson that helps students achieve the highest rating on the rubric look like and how do I need to change my lessons to be more effective? Can I see it work with my students? How do I teach the lessons listed on the curriculum map? How do I use the knowledge gained from analyzing student work to develop a series of lessons to meet my students' needs? Talking and reading about teaching and learning does not simply translate into more effective teaching and learning for most people, at least not for me. I need to watch a demonstration, ideally with my students or students similar to mine; give it a try with someone's support; get immediate, in-the-moment feedback; analyze what works and what doesn't; and then try it again. I want to attend professional development sessions that not only increase my knowledge but, as important, improve my skills.

And, as a literacy coach, I want to plan and lead professional development sessions that actually lead to the improvement of teaching and learning. Would this session, I think to myself, help my teachers drive the car safely?

Plan Based on Teacher Needs and Determine a Focus That Increases Teacher Knowledge and Skill

When you design professional development sessions that focus on increasing teacher knowledge and skill, you can begin by asking yourself a series of questions:

◆ Of all the things that we could work on, and based on classroom observations, analysis of student data, conversations with my principal, conversations with other principals, prior work with teachers, and my knowledge of literacy, what is within my teachers' zone of proximal development and what will move teachers forward in their practice?

◆ What do I want teachers to know and be able to do as a result of the professional development session? To make sure your purpose is specific enough for the session, ask yourself, What will start to look different in classrooms tomorrow as a result of this session?

◆ How much time do I have for the session? When can I have follow-up sessions? The amount of time you have for your professional study helps you determine the scope of your focus.

One Coach's Process of Determining a Focus

To see how the questions can help determine a clear focus for professional development sessions, follow the planning process a school-based coach, Vicky Holeman, and I used. We began by working together to identify a focus for the session based on her teachers' needs.

KATHERINE: What do you want your teachers to know?

VICKY: I want my teachers to know about the value of accountable talk. The district is focusing on accountable talk and teachers have asked me for more help in understanding the district focus. Based on what I see in classrooms, I agree that we need to get students actively engaged in the lessons. So many of our students seem so passive in their learning. A few students dominate the lessons and the rest of the students don't get engaged in the discussions we have about texts or they just seem to be waiting for teachers to tell them what to do.

KATHERINE: What do you want your teachers to be able to do as a result of the session?

VICKY: I want them to use accountable talk strategies, but I know that is really vague. Can you help me get more specific?

KATHERINE: Sure. How much time do you have for the session?

VICKY: I have two hours for this particular session. We also have a forty-five minute meeting scheduled next week. I plan to keep working on accountable talk when we have professional development sessions during the next two months.

KATHERINE: I'm relieved to hear you have two hours with follow-up sessions already on the calendar. To get more specific in my planning, I try to envision how teaching and learning may begin to shift as a result of professional development. What do you hope will look different in classrooms tomorrow as a result of your professional development session?

VICKY: When I visit classrooms I'd like to hear every student making meaning of texts. I'd like to think that teachers would be trying to use accountable talk strategies.

KATHERINE: What do you mean by accountable talk strategies?

VICKY: Well, I guess I don't mean things like having students say, "I agree, I disagree, I want to add on . . ." because we tried that and students just mimic the language. Here's what I observe. Right now what I see is teachers asking pretty surface-level questions. For example, when they are talking about stories, regardless of the grade level, I hear teachers asking students questions like, "Who are the characters? What is the setting?" I want them asking questions like, "Are these characters believable? How is the setting influencing the character's decisions? Why might the characters be acting this way?" I think the literal questions make it impossible for the students to have rich discussions. So I want to focus on helping teachers craft and use more provocative questions with students to help students make meaning of the text instead of just skimming the surface. Also, when students respond, I hear teachers saying, "Good answer." Or, "No . . . does anyone have another answer?" I'm not hearing teachers say things like, "What makes you say that?" to get inside the students' thinking. I'm not hearing other students say things like, "Help me understand how you got that idea." So the teachers' responses aren't promoting thinking and discussion. I'd like to focus on showing teachers ways to probe student thinking so that students can learn how to think deeply about texts. And I'd like to hear teachers probing for student thinking when I visit classrooms.

KATHERINE: I find if we can understand why things are the way they are, we can begin to problem-solve how to make changes. Why do you think teachers are currently doing what they're doing—asking surface-level story-element questions and responding with "good answer"?

VICKY: I think teachers are doing what they know how to do and what they think they should be doing. At every grade level teachers are working on narrative texts right now with an emphasis on story elements, but the work doesn't seem to get increasingly more challenging. Maybe I haven't done enough work with them on how the complexity of the work should increase from K–6. So I play a part in why I'm seeing teachers doing what they're doing. During my own education, the role of my teachers was to let me know when I was correct or incorrect. Many of the teachers with whom I work now are recognizing that the role of the teacher is shifting, but it is challenging to shift from saying "Good answer" to "What makes you say that?" I know that I'm really working hard to shift my own instruction to include responses that probe for more, so I know it is easier said than done.

KATHERINE: Now that we've talked a bit, what do you want your teachers to know and be able to do as a result of your professional development session?

VICKY: Well, I know the focus of the session isn't a vague or generic look at accountable talk anymore! I want my teachers to know that for students to become engaged in meaning-making discussions about texts, we need to shift the questions and responses we are using. I'd like my teachers to gain experience with questioning strategies that help students go beyond the surface level of the text. Maybe we can look at the standards at various grade levels to see what students are expected to be doing with story elements. I'd also like my teachers to begin to understand the power of responding to students with questions like "What are you thinking? What makes you say that? Can you explain to us how you arrived at that idea? What in the text or what in our conversation makes you think that?" instead of "Good answer" or "Nope . . . does anyone else have an answer?"

KATHERINE: We've shifted your focus from "accountable talk" to a narrower focus on questioning strategies and responding strategies that help students better understand the texts they're reading. Let's just make sure your narrower focus is within your teachers' zone of proximal development. Based on what you know about your teachers, does this focus make sense?

VICKY: Yes, it makes a lot more sense than just "accountable talk." I can imagine teachers walking away from the session with something that they can immediately apply to their teaching and that the changes have the potential to be quite dramatic. Now I just have to figure out how to structure the two hours I have with them.

When I reread the transcript of our conversation, I applaud how Vicky worked hard to become much more concrete about the focus of her professional development session. Envisioning the changes that could take place in classrooms helped both of us get a clearer sense of what is currently happening in classrooms and why, what makes sense to work on as a group of educators to help shift instruction, and what can be accomplished realistically during the professional development session.

Design the Session to Meet the Needs of the Teachers

Once you have a clearer focus, brainstorm a variety of ways to structure the session to meet the needs of the teachers. The process of planning for professional development will help you further clarify your focus when you get specific about what and how you plan to teach during the session. Remember to refer back to your notes about what your teachers reported they need for their learning such as demonstration lessons, professional texts to read, materials to use with students, or time to process information with colleagues, so that you keep your teachers' requests in mind. The following questions can help you keep in mind that adult learners benefit from professional development sessions that incorporate Cambourne's conditions of learning and follow a gradual release of responsibility framework.

- ◆ How can I structure the session to accomplish the purpose and to meet the needs of the teachers?
  - How can I structure the session to enable a gradual release of responsibility?
    - To—What will be explicitly modeled and demonstrated?
    - With—What will the teachers do *with* me that they can then do *without* me?

- By—What will the teachers do by themselves as I observe and provide feedback and response during the session so that they feel confident trying on the work in their classrooms?
  - How will I address the conditions of learning?
    - Immersion—In what will I immerse teachers?
    - Demonstration—What will be explicitly demonstrated and why? By whom? With whom?
    - Expectation—How can I communicate my expectations that all teachers will be successful?
    - Responsibility—What is the rationale for the learning and how will teachers take responsibility for taking on the learning?
    - Practice or Use—What opportunities will teachers have during the session and in their classrooms to use or practice the learning?
    - Approximation—What opportunities will teachers have during the session and in their classrooms to approximate the learning?
    - Response—How will I provide the necessary feedback and response to support teachers in their learning?
    - Engagement—What will promote teacher engagement during the session?

One Coach's Designing Process

Let's go back to my conversation with Vicky to see how she grappled with how to design an effective professional development session.

KATHERINE: Vicky, based on what you hope teachers will know and be able to do, how do you plan to structure the two hours you have with your teachers?

VICKY: I want to start by honoring that teachers are working hard to craft lessons that reflect our focus on story element work within narrative texts. I've taken photos of teachers reading aloud narrative texts and of students' written responses to the read-alouds so that I can post the photos and writing around the room as a celebration of our work. And then I have to figure out a way to help people see that their lessons could be improved to take students further in their learning. Remember how you asked me why teachers are teaching the way they are? That question made me remember that we teach the best way we know how and if we're expected to change our practice, we need to be made aware in a way that makes sense that changes need to happen. So how can I help people see that they can improve their lessons with different questions and responses?

KATHERINE: Think about yourself as a learner. What would need to happen for you to become aware that you can improve your teaching?

VICKY: I'd need to compare what I'm already doing with the suggested improvements, I guess. I'd be curious about what makes the improvements that much better.

KATHERINE: So, what do you think your teachers need for their learning so that they can compare what they're already doing with what you're suggesting they try?

VICKY: I'm thinking I should split the teachers into two groups and have half assume the role of students and the other [half] as observers and scripters of the lesson. I'll let everyone know that we'll be focusing on the responses to students and the questions I ask to get students thinking about the story elements. In the first lesson [about ten minutes] I'll teach a lesson that resembles what I am seeing in classrooms. I'll use the story element questions I'm hearing teachers ask and their responses to student ideas, too. My teachers said it is really helpful when I chart ideas, so I'd like to debrief the lesson and fill out the left side of two charts (*shows charts*):

Responding to Students	
Responses to students in the first lesson	Responses to students in the second lesson

Questioning About Story Elements	
Questions in the first lesson	Questions in the second lesson

VICKY: Then I'd like to teach the same lesson with the same text, this time using questioning strategies and responses that open the door to more student thinking and talk. That way I can take people from where they are in their practice to seeing the possibilities of where they can go. After the second lesson, I'll have people fill in the other side of the two charts. I'd like teachers to talk about what made the second lesson more effective at teaching students how to make meaning of texts. It would be even more powerful to have videos of me teaching two lessons to students, but since our professional development session is in two days, there is no way I can find the time to make the videos.

KATHERINE: What will they take away from the session to try in their own classrooms?

VICKY: I'll start by asking teachers what they find valuable from the session to try on with their students. And I'll ask teachers to look at the responses and questions we charted and decide which two or few they will try on in their own teaching. I'll have index cards available so that they can write them down and use them as they teach. I'll ask them to come back to professional development next week and share how their questions and responses affected student talk and student understanding. I've also scheduled coaching time in one of the teacher's rooms for early next week. If it makes sense in our coaching work, we can try on this work together and perhaps even videotape the lessons to share with the group. We'll see. I may be getting ahead of myself!

After Vicky and I talked about her professional development plan, we got specific about what would actually happen during the professional development session using a planning sheet (Figure 7–5) based on Cambourne's conditions of learning. As we worked on the planning sheet, we continued to clarify the purpose of the professional development session. While it looks like a great deal of work to plan for one session, because Vicky is a relatively new literacy coach, spending time on planning helps her feel confident about her work with her teachers. As Vicky plans and delivers more professional development sessions, her thought processes will become automatic and her planning time will speed up. When I cautioned Vicky not to get discouraged about the amount of time the planning process takes, she voiced what I've often experienced: "I'd rather spend more time planning a well-crafted session than wing it and spend days, weeks, and maybe even months cleaning up the mess I could create by wasting my teachers' time in a haphazard session."

1. Date of professional development: November 3, 2005

2. Who is involved? *(whole staff, a particular department, a particular grade level, etc.)* For how long?

Whole staff—K to fifth grade for two hours.

3. What do I want my teachers to know? *(content)*

I want my teachers to know that in order to engage our students in meaning-making discussions about texts, we need to shift our questioning and response strategies.

4. What do I want my teachers to be able to do? *(application)*

I want my teachers to be able to try on questions about stories that help students think critically about texts. I want my teachers to probe for understanding when students give responses.

5. As you plan, think about the eight areas of the conditions of learning

Immersion—*Teachers need to be immersed in the work.*

This is the first of a few sessions on working to engage all of our students in meaning-making discussions about texts. Teachers will be immersed in scripting and/or participating in lessons to get the feel for the questioning strategies.

Since some of my teachers always ask for research, I have an article copied for people to take with them. Ketch, A. (2005, September). "Conversation: The Comprehension Connection." *The Reading Teacher*, 59 (1), 8–13.

Demonstration—*Teachers need to see many demonstrations of how to do what you want them to do.*

I plan to do two demonstration lessons. The first will resemble lessons I see in classrooms. Because I don't want teachers to think I'm mocking them or setting them up, I am going to be clear about my intentions: we'll look at my two lessons to analyze the effect of questioning and probing for more on student learning. The second will demonstrate using more provocative questions and will model ways to respond to student comments that probe for understanding.

Engagement—*Teachers need to believe that they can do what you are showing them, it is useful to them, and they feel secure enough to risk trying both in the session and afterward.*

I want to teach lessons that elevate what teachers are already trying to do with their students—teach students to comprehend narrative texts with a close eye on story elements. Because I am choosing familiar lessons to demonstrate, I hope teachers believe the work is aligned with their work and is doable in their classrooms.

FIG. 7–5 Planning for professional development

Expectation—*Teachers are more likely to try on/engage in the work when your expectations for them to implement their learning are explicit and clear.*

Charting the questions and responses should make the work clear. Also, having teachers write down on index cards the questions and prompts they want to try and then letting teachers know that we'll have time to follow up on how trying on the work went in classrooms at our next session should help make the expectations clear.

Responsibility—*Teachers need to make decisions about how, when, and how often to try on new learning to improve instruction.*

Responsibility is built into the session when teachers decide which questions and responses they want to try on.

Practice—*Teachers need time and opportunity to use and practice their developing skills in meaningful ways.*

Teachers won't have a chance during this session to actually practice the questioning and response strategies on students since the session is after school. Instead, they'll practice in their classrooms and then report how the work went.

They will get practice listening for the questioning and response strategies when they participate in the lessons and will have time to practice analyzing the effect of the strategies on the meaning-making opportunities in the lesson.

Approximation—*Teachers must be free to approximate the desired model. Mistakes are essential for learning.*

Approximation will happen in people's classrooms. During the next session, I expect that we'll probably co-plan a lesson together that aims to engage all students in meaningful conversation about texts. My teachers request co-planning time and that will be a great venue for people practicing and approximating planning for conversation. I also plan to work with one teacher next week in a gradual release coaching cycle and I anticipate practice and approximation will be part of our work together.

Response—*Feedback is an essential part of learning. Feedback needs to be relevant and appropriate.*

At our next professional development session we'll start with sharing how the work went in classrooms. If someone decides to videotape, that will give us another rich opportunity to respond and provide feedback.

6. How am I going to check for understanding?

There are a few built-in places to check for understanding: when teachers co-construct the two charts, during the compare and contrast discussion, when teachers decide what to try on in their classrooms, and their exit slips.

FIG. 7–5 Cont.

Checking for Understanding

In order to be responsive to teachers' needs during a professional development session, you need to build in opportunities to check for understanding. Listen in on the conversations teachers have during partner talk, as they work collaboratively in small groups, or in whole-group discussions. Read the comments they post in the "parking lot." Build in opportunities for reflective writing and listen as participants share their ideas with others. Encourage participants to ask questions throughout your session. Think aloud about questions you anticipate participants may be hesitant to ask: "You may be wondering how you'll figure out how to organize your conferring notes with thirty-five students in your class. Is anyone wondering about this?"

Consider using exit slips at the end of a session or portion of an all-day session to check for understanding. I like feedback on the content, the structure of the session, and next steps, and I leave space comments or further suggestions. My prompts ask about:

- The content
  - Share two important ideas from today's work.
  - What challenged your thinking today?
  - What ideas or questions do you plan to consider further?
- The structure of the session
  - What worked well in the session today?
  - How can the next session be improved?
- Next steps
  - What do you plan to use from this session in the upcoming days?
  - What are your next steps?
  - What should we do next to continue our learning?
  - What do you need next from your colleagues?
  - How can I support you?

 ## Concrete Ideas About the Gradual Release of Responsibility

Ideas About the To

When using a gradual release of responsibility framework in designing professional development, moving through the to-with-by, we can think of the *to* as the time when we provide teachers with a information about the improvement of instruction. We provide:

◆ *Urgency*—by using student data and information about why practice needs to improve to meet student needs

◆ *Rationale* for why we've chosen to address this particular topic in professional development and which students will benefit from this work

◆ *An agenda* listing what we will work to accomplish in professional development, how we plan to accomplish it, and time frames for accomplishing it

◆ *Demonstration and modeling* of a particular way of teaching or doing something

◆ *Examples* to create a visual of what we're talking about (using video, or sample texts, or lesson plans, or transcripts, or student work)

◆ *Expectations* about what we expect to see in classrooms as a result of our work together

The purpose of the *to* is to get information said, read, watched, or discussed. The coach is on the *giving* end and the teachers are on the *receiving* end of the information. While the teacher may be actively involved, the mode teachers are in during the *to* is, "Tell me what you need me to know, show me what you're talking about, bring me up to speed."

Some teachers spend their energy turning whatever is said during the *to* into direct implications for their classrooms. They see the relevance to their teaching, can visualize what it would mean for their teaching, and are willing to give it a try. Usually they can turn ideas into action quickly because the ideas address a point of need in their teaching.

Some teachers spend their energy listening to what is being presented and working to make sense of it all, leaving little energy for visualizing classroom instruction. However, because they have just received lots of information, they may feel full of great ideas and, in that state of excitement about having new information, believe they know how to transfer the learning back into the classroom. When asked, "What does this mean for your classroom?" they can, in the moment, say exactly what it means for instruction. But saying what it means and doing what it means are two entirely different things.

Others in the room will think they know what the coach is trying to teach them. Everyone makes their own meaning of text—and oral communication is text—and we have all experienced the phenomenon of people saying, "But I heard you say I should do that in my classroom" and what they are saying they understand from your professional development is not at all what you meant for them to understand. As a result, some of the people who can quickly turn professional development into changes in the classroom are actually practicing things you did not mean for them to practice. And then when you work to undo those ineffective practices, you are met with resentment because teachers believe you wanted them to work in the very way you now want them to change.

Still others just do not learn well in the receptive mode because of their learning style or because they need repeated experiences with the material. Much of what is said, shown, discussed, or viewed during the *to* does not start to make sense until people are asked to engage in co-construction of something. As they work, these teachers will often be heard saying, "Oh, is that what she meant by . . ." or "Now I get what she was talking about." Co-construction is the only way this group of teachers will start to internalize and transfer things from the *to* into practice. Without the co-construction opportunities, the *to* literally falls on deaf ears.

If we skip to the *by* at this point, this is what we can expect to see in classrooms:

◆ Nothing new—from those who do not learn well in the receptive mode

◆ Frustration—from those who thought they "got it" but cannot actually make "it" happen because the session focused on knowledge without emphasizing skill

◆ Enthusiasm and then anger—from those who are trying what they *thought* you said you wanted and now are being "corrected"

◆ Genuine enthusiasm and beginning success—from those who did get what you were saying, changed instruction accordingly, and are being successful

How many people actually fit into that last category? Very few. And they are rarely the people who need to make dramatic changes to their instruction.

Ideas About the With

Going back to the list of how people respond to the *to*, it is clear why moving to the *with* is so crucial. Everybody on that list will learn more and better from engaging in co-construction of meaning. At the very least, those in the "genuine enthusiasm" category will have multiple opportunities to refine their learning. At the very most, the "nothing new" category will start to hear and understand what is being said as they co-construct knowledge. The "frustration" group will see the work is challenging for everyone and will get the opportunity to hear the ideas again, fill in the missing pieces, or get over the stumbling block. And hopefully the number of people in the "enthusiasm and then anger" group will be smaller because one goal of the *with* is to check for understanding, clarify confusion, and solidify good practices to avoid ever having people go back and practice poor instruction.

During the *with* we need to provide *multiple* opportunities for people to engage in co-constructed learning. But we need to be careful about how quickly we release responsibility to the teachers.

◆ How overwhelming is the task for the teacher?
◆ What challenges can be removed so that learning can take place?
◆ What aspects of the task can be held in common by the whole group so that people can learn from each other?

For example, planning a lesson is such a complex task: assessing student needs, designing a focus to meet the needs, selecting a text or task to support the teachers and demonstrate the focus, designing an effective lesson, anticipating student outcomes, and so on. While teachers need to learn how to do all those parts, is it possible to learn all of the parts at once? Unlikely.

I think of planning the *with* as a balance of controlling some variables to allow for grappling with others. I think of my driver's ed teacher letting me first drive on neighborhood streets with four-way stop signs before letting me drive on busy streets with yield signs near the local strip mall.

To support lesson planning, I might provide a profile of the students' strengths and areas of need, predetermine the learning outcome or instructional focus for the lesson, and select the text so that the work the teachers do together can be on designing an effective lesson. This way everyone in the room is talking about the same students, same focus, and same text so that we can analyze and discuss the different ways people approach designing the lesson. When I do not provide small groups with a common task, then the groups do not have the basis for common conversation and co-construction and discussion is scattered and focused on, "This is what we decided to teach, the text we decided to use, how we designed the lesson," and the listeners, who do not have the same focus, are unfamiliar with the text, and did not try to design that lesson, have no real reason to care about what is being said. In a more supported (controlled) experience, the discussion can be "We are all trying to accomplish the same goal with the same materials—this is the way we decided to conduct the lesson and why. What do you think of our decisions?" The listeners can compare what is being said with the decisions they made. Discussion about the differences in the decisions provides additional opportunities for learning.

With experiences must be planned if teachers are going to learn how to engage in complex work. By controlling some aspects of the *with*, teachers have a chance to improve their knowledge and skill with parts. This does not mean teachers are ready to tackle everything. More *with* is needed to support their learning of the previously controlled aspects, working toward knowledge and skill of the whole task.

When aspects of the learning are controlled, teachers are more successful and the temptation is to think, "They got it! Fantastic! Now I can expect to see it in classrooms!" Always keep in mind what the "it" actually is. At first, the "it" is a relatively small portion of the whole concept—whatever you chose to have people grapple with. Over time, as you release more responsibility, the "it" becomes an increasingly larger portion of the whole concept. If you decide to look for evidence in classrooms, look only for evidence of exactly what learning you supported. Also keep in mind that learning can be elusive and slippery. How often are you able to do something one day that you cannot do the very next day, for whatever reason? Remember that repetition is essential for learning.

Ideas About the Gradual Release

The gradual release is not done in lockstep (Figure 7–6), starting with the coach thinking aloud, demonstrating, and doing all of the work while participants passively listen for an entire session, reserving the collaborative

Design of a session earlier in the work	Design of a session as the work progresses	Design of a session as the work has taken hold
To	With	By

FIG. 7–6 Misapplication of the gradual release in sessions

and co-constructed experiences for another session. How deadly would that be?

Rather than each session having equal doses of *to*, *with*, and *by*, think of gradual release as a fluid process of providing information, having participants grapple in small groups or individually, bringing the group together for more information, and grappling yet again. Think about successive sessions about the same topic as having increasing amounts of *with* and *by* and decreasing amounts of *to* as learning builds (see Figure 7–7).

Examine the descriptions of the two sessions on guided reading in Figures 7–8 and 7–9 to better understand how the gradual release of responsibility may look in successive sessions. Rather than telling participants all about guided reading in upper-grade classrooms, I wanted participants in the first session engaged in constructing a beginning understanding of guided reading by viewing, analyzing, and discussing a guided reading lesson, naming what they learned about students as readers, and comparing the video to ideas in a professional text. The participants cannot be expected to go off and try guided reading in their own classrooms because the purpose and design of the session falls squarely in the *to*, or "I do, you watch" stage of guided release.

Notice how I continue to build an understanding of guided reading in the second session by engaging participants in modified lesson study. Now what are the participants doing with their colleagues and me that they may be able to do in their classrooms?

Design of a session earlier in the work	Design of a session as the work progresses	Design of a session as the work has taken hold
TO	TO	TO
WITH	WITH	WITH
BY	BY	BY

FIG. 7–7 Gradual release of responsibility within and across sessions

Guiding Questions	Tasks	Expected Outcomes
How do student needs inform guided reading planning?	Prior to watching a guided reading video, participants review the lesson plan, hear about the students as learners, and read the selected text. Participants hear from the literacy coach the planning and considerations that went into planning the lesson.	Participants hear the careful planning and thoughtful consideration of student needs that precede teaching a lesson.
What can guided reading look like in the upper grades? What is the role of teacher talk? Student talk? What is supporting the students' meaning making?	Participants break into groups of four and assign themselves observation roles to focus video viewing: • One participant scripts teacher language. • Each remaining participant selects one or two students to watch and take notes on. During the viewing, the coach stops the video to process what has been seen so far.	Participants get a visual of what upper-grade guided reading can look like. Participants observe how guided reading supports students' meaning making of instructional level texts.
What can we learn about students as readers during guided reading?	After viewing the video, participants discuss what they saw, addressing the guiding questions. Participants are encouraged to use tangible evidence—like notes taken during the lesson—to justify what is being said. Ex: What did you hear that student say that leads you to conclude . . . or What did the teacher say to promote that talk?	Various aspects of the lesson are analyzed so that participants can see the power of questioning, prompting, student talk, and observing students.
	Participants discuss how the observed lesson challenges or confirms the ideas they gathered from reading from the first chapter of *A Closer Look at Guided Reading* by David Hornsby prior to the session.	Participants revise their understanding of guided reading.

FIG. 7–8 First guided reading session

Guiding Questions	Tasks	Expected Outcomes
How do student needs inform guided reading planning?	Prior to watching a video of a guided reading lesson being conducted with students with strengths and areas of need similar to participants' students, participants review the lesson plan, hear about the students as learners, and read the selected text. Participants review their student data (conferring notes and other assessments) to identify students in their class with similar strengths and areas of need.	Participants practice analyzing their own student data to inform instruction.
What can guided reading look like in the upper grades? What is the role of teacher talk? Student talk? What is supporting the students' meaning making?	Participants determine their observation roles in groups of four. • One participant writes down the questions the teacher asks, the prompts the teacher gives, and any other teacher moves. • Other participants select one or two students to watch and take notes on.	Participants get a another visual of what upper-grade guided reading can look like. Participants observe once again how guided reading supports students' meaning making of instructional level texts.
How do we use what we learn about students in one lesson to inform the next lesson?	After watching the video, each small group debriefs the lesson, discussing what they learned about students as readers. Teachers consider ways to improve the lesson to better support students in constructing meaning. Together the whole group revises the lesson plan to improve aspects that were not as effective, and selects a teacher to voice their co-constructed lesson.	Participants co-plan and revise a lesson. Participants design appropriate questions, determine where to chunk texts, and how to introduce and close a lesson to support student meaning making. *Continues*

FIG. 7–9 Second guided reading session

Guiding Questions	Tasks	Expected Outcomes
What can we learn about students as readers during guided reading?	Students arrive and a second teacher implements the lesson plan (with the same observation structure as above).	Participants observe a variety of student reading behaviors and use those observations to inform decision making.
How can learning from lesson study help shape our lesson planning to meet student needs?	The group processes the success of their revisions using evidence of student learning such as observation notes and makes additional revisions to the plan. Group members commit to trying the lesson with similar group of students and returning with their reflections next session.	Participants are now familiar with a lesson and a text and are expected to try it with their students. Participants are asked to do the *by* in their classrooms (either with the support of a colleague or coach) so that the group can learn from everyone's experiences (and so that the individuals can practice and individualize what was just learned).

FIG. 7–9 Cont.

Be Transparent with Your Decision Making

The professional development sessions you design for teachers provide you with crucial opportunities to model your beliefs about teaching and learning. Your teachers may learn as much about how to teach their students from how you teach them as from what you tell them about teaching. The old adage "Actions speak louder than words" prevails once again. When your sessions are planned based on their needs; when you teach and lead sessions while checking for understanding and being a responsive teacher and making necessary adjustments to your session; and when you clearly structure the next learning opportunity because you have reflected on evidence of their learning, your teachers will begin to know the power of effective instruction. Be acutely aware that your message must be evidenced in your teaching; otherwise, your sessions may inadvertently reinforce ineffective teaching. For example, if you advocate high levels of engagement in classrooms and you have teachers sit and listen during the bulk of your sessions, what message are you really sending?

I use my agendas to be as transparent as possible not only about what and how we are going to learn together, but also about the guiding questions that frame my decision making. Take a look in Figure 7–10 at how explicit I try to be about the content and structure of the session in my agenda.

As well planned as you try to be going into a session, remain keenly aware that being responsive to your students' needs is essential to effective teaching. Make notes on your copy of the agenda about how you adjust the

Time	What do we want partici-pants to know and be able to do?	How will we get them there?	Materials
8:00–8:15	Establish goal for the session—To provide teachers with a beginning understanding of conferring Guiding questions: • What can conferring look like and sound like? • What is the purpose of conferring? • What systems do teachers use to keep track of conferring notes? • What do you plan to use from today's session in your classroom?		
8:15–8:30	Do: Engage in self-assessment to determine level of knowl-edge about conferring.	Quick-write—What do you already know about conferring? What are two questions you have about conferring? Place questions in the middle of your table so I can review them.	Large index cards
8:30–9:00	Know: What can conferring look like and sound like?	View 3 conferring videos—Carlos, Olga, and Joanne. Analyze—what did you notice about the conferring process? Discuss your noticings with a partner.	Videos of three fifth graders Conferring notes for each student *Continues*

FIG. 7–10 Agenda: *A closer look at conferring*—a session for third- to fifth-grade teachers

Time	What do we want participants to know and be able to do?	How will we get them there?	Materials
9:00– 9:10	Know: What is the architecture of conferring?	As a group, let's discuss the structure I used each time I conferred. What did you notice about the structure?	Overhead of Calkins quote from p. 102
9:10– 9:45	Know: What is the purpose of conferring?	Read first section of Chapter 6, "Coaching and Conferring with Readers" from *The Art of Teaching Reading*. Use sticky notes to jot ideas for discussion in the margin. Discuss ideas with the teachers at your table.	*The Art of Teaching Reading* Sticky notes
9:45– 10:00	Break		
10:00– 10:30	Know: How do teachers keep track of conferring?	Examine a variety of conferring systems to begin to understand how to keep track of information	Four teachers' conferring notes
10:30– 11:00	Do: Plan how to begin to confer.	Make a plan for how you will keep track of student information and when you may begin to confer.	
11:00– 11:15	Do: Reflect on today's session and provide feedback.	Look back at the two questions you had about conferring. If one or both of your questions remain, park them in the blue pocket chart on your way out. Complete the exit slip.	Exit slips Blue pocket chart "parking lot"

FIG. 7–10 Cont.

session, perhaps by lengthening a section, doing more think-aloud, changing the guiding question, or addressing an unanticipated concern, so that after the session you can learn from those adjustments.

 ## Adding Value

See what I mean about the potential of professional development workshops and sessions? Everything we do can add value with careful planning and facilitation. When you're not sure about which direction to head in with adult learners, ask them what they need for their learning and check back with authentic learning experiences in which you learned to do something well. If you don't like what you accomplish in one session, use the feedback you get to inform your decision making for the next session. The good news about being involved in an ongoing coaching relationship with teachers is that you have multiple opportunities to continue on the journey of honing your craft as you help your teachers hone theirs.

The Promise of Coaching

"Writing workshop just doesn't work!" groaned Grace, a first-grade teacher of English Language Learners. Her literacy coach and I were equally frustrated by our inability to help her meet the needs of her students through a series of co-planned lessons. Grace had tried everything she learned during professional development and by reading professional texts to get writing workshop up and running, but nothing seemed to be working. Her students could not seem to find their own writing ideas. Grace lamented, "Maybe my colleagues are correct. Maybe writing workshop just doesn't work with my kind of students. Maybe all they can do, or all *I* can get them to do, is write to a prompt."

Not wanting Grace to give up on using the workshop approach, her coach and I tried to support her any way she needed. We co-planned a few more lessons and brainstormed strategies for engaging the students in their writing. Still highly skeptical, Grace said she would be willing to give writing workshop a few more attempts and agreed to side-by-side teach with her coach for the remainder of the week—mostly because it was already on her schedule.

On Friday I stopped by Grace's room as part of a scheduled intravisitation. A dozen primary teachers, the principal, and a few central office people sat scattered around the room to watch students at work on their writing. What a sight it was to find Grace surrounded by students who were now clamoring to share their writing ideas with her. Finally, all the teaching and coaching had paid off: Grace's students had found their writers' voices. Just as I spotted her, Grace looked over at her coach and mouthed, "We did it! Look at what my students can do!" Knowing how hard Grace and her coach had worked to get to this point, I couldn't stop my eyes from welling up with tears. One of Grace's first graders looked up at me. "You look like Rudolph the red-nosed reindeer," she remarked, her high-pitched voice cutting through the din of students chatting as they wrote. Rats. Had my Rudolph nose given me away again? A running joke in my family since childhood, my nose indicates when the temperature is really cold or, more embarrassingly, when I am getting emotional. "Your nose is all red," continued the first grader, "are you crying about something? Hey, everyone, Ms. Casey is sad!"

Writing came to a halt and everyone, students and visitors, turned to look at me. Though I just wanted to savor Grace's triumphant joy, I knew if I didn't respond quickly, I'd have a crowd of six-year-olds rushing over to comfort me, so I fibbed, "I'm OK. I just have something in my eye." The first graders bought my excuse: the adults glanced over, unconvinced.

The moment I witnessed between Grace and her coach symbolizes for me the power of literacy coaching to transform student learning. Worried about keeping pace with her colleagues and meeting her grade-level's benchmark targets, Grace admitted that, without her coach's support, she would have lost faith in her teaching and in her students' ability to be expressive writers. Our beliefs about our literacy teaching are shaped not by what we read in professional texts or observe others do, but by the everyday interactions we have with children, every time we look for signs that they are learning because of our teaching. We are easily frustrated when our initial attempts at trying on new instructional practices are not immediately successful in the ways we want them to be, and it is too tempting to revert to how we've always taught. We need to be surrounded by educators who boost our confidence and guide us as we apply new knowledge and skill to transform our teaching.

My Rudolph nose shows up a lot these days as I gather with teachers and literacy coaches in classrooms or in professional development sessions, all of us working alongside each other to figure out how to ensure all students are learning. There's something quite magical, right, and yet rare about educators working side-by-side to change instruction together. I find the promise of literacy coaching deeply moving.

In these times, in which it is critical to validate everything we do with research, we literacy coaches are doing our jobs day in and day out without research's seal of approval. Studies of our form of professional development are scant. Are the underpinnings of literacy coaching—grounded in inquiry, collaborative, ongoing, intensive, supported by modeling and collective problem solving, connected to teachers' work with their students—supported by research? Certainly. It is just that "no one, as yet, has proven that coaching contributes significantly to increased student achievement" (Neufeld and

Roper 2003). As we do our jobs well, as we work to increase student learning, we are poised to become the subjects of research studies that will validate our work.

I end with some of the many voices of educators and students that echoed in my mind throughout the writing of this book. They, and countless others working together every day in schools, are why we coach. Their voices are rich with the promise coaching can bring.

Let's listen to Lisa Young, a seventh-grade teacher at Gompers Charter Middle School.

> Going through the coaching cycle was an experience that allowed me to be a part of my coach's understanding of teaching. The whole process was powerful, but teaching side-by-side with my coach was the part that really made a difference in my lessons. I was able to watch the precise moves she made, and feel the pace and presence she had in the classroom. My coach has a way of listening to the students to assess exactly where they are with regard to the purpose of her lesson and their learning. I learned so much as she guided me through this assessment with my own students. Receiving feedback from my coach throughout the process was very important to me because I felt confident that I could take all I learned into my own teaching. My students are surprising me with all they are learning.

Los Alisos Middle School sixth-grade teacher Sofia Garcia's voice reminds us that when we affect one teacher's practice, we affect hundreds of students' learning.

> I never thought that it was possible to get to know each of my seventy-five plus students. There seemed to be too many barriers, especially such short class periods. Though I considered myself a good teacher, understanding my students' needs was an aspect of teaching that I didn't know I should do or even how to do. I wasn't ready to try to customize my lessons for all the different students in my class. I simply thought that I should teach to the state standards and that I was doing my job. The only problem with that is that all of my students were at completely different levels. Some of my students were struggling with decoding while others were fluent readers.
> My literacy coach taught me how to identify the needs of students through various assessments including writing, reading interviews, conferring, analyzing data, and observations during read-alouds. I was amazed at how quickly I was able to get to know my students' needs through these methods. My coach helped me figure out what

to teach students next, how to customize my lessons, and showed me how to have conversations with students about their next steps so they could focus their learning.

The strategies my coach taught me will forever change how I educate my students now and for years to come. Now it's all about meeting my students' needs, preparing them for their future, and enjoying it along the way.

And here's Jacob, a fourth grader I met when his teacher and I worked in a gradual release coaching cycle together last spring.

Dear Ms. Casey,

I'm writing you a thank you note because I want to say thank you. I learned a lot when you worked with my teacher and us on our reading. At first I thought you were weird. You asked us hard questions and made us talk a lot and you made my head hurt. But then after a couple of days I noticed I felt smarter about my reading. My friends said they did, too. I think it is because we had a two-headed teacher. You taught us and my teacher taught us at the same time. That was cool. Sometimes you sounded just like my teacher and sometimes she sounded just like you, like you were trading your brains back and forth to each other. You know what the best part of it was? My teacher smiled a lot when we did good work. She says she's proud of us. I think she's proud of herself, too, and that's why she's smiling. I never knew that teachers can teach each other. I hope you're smiling, too.

Love,
Jacob

I do smile whenever I read Jacob's note (looking like Rudolph every time). The work of teaching and learning, the work of literacy coaching, is among the most challenging work we can do, making the results all the more satisfying. We teach our children when they are young that promises are meant to be kept. It is up to us to fulfill the promise of coaching. Our students are counting on us.

Annotated Bibliography

've separated this annotated bibliography into sections that reflect some of the big areas in which literacy coaches need to have knowledge. What follows in not an exhaustive bibliography; instead, here are the titles I turn to first when I, or teachers with whom I am working, need additional information and support.

 ## How Smart Readers Construct Meaning of Texts

When I work with teachers, the question of what it means to teach students to comprehend texts comes up repeatedly. What are the comprehension strategies smart readers use to construct meaning? Our conversations often focus on how to teach students to move beyond word calling or skimming the surface of the text and into constructing meaning for the texts. By reading texts and becoming aware of what I do as a reader to make meaning, I've realized that I need to strengthen my own comprehension of texts. For example, after reading about comprehension strategies, interpretation, and critical literacy in professional texts and applying the strategies to my own reading, I'm becoming a much more thoughtful and critical reader. You can use the ideas in these professional texts to enhance not only the teaching of reading, but also your and your teachers' reading lives.

Beck, Isabel L., Margaret G. McKeown, Rebecca L. Hamilton, and Linda Kucan. 1997. *Questioning the Author: An Approach for Enhancing Student Engagement with Text.* Newark, DE: International Reading Association.

Harvey, Stephanie, and **Anne Goudvis.** 2000. *Strategies That Work: Teaching Comprehension to Enhance Understanding.* Portland, ME: Stenhouse.

Keene, Ellin Oliver, and **Susan Zimmerman.** 1997. *Mosaic of Thought: Teaching Comprehension in a Reader's Workshop*. Portsmouth, NH: Heinemann.

McLaughlin, Maureen, and **Glenn DeVoogd.** 2004. *Critical Literacy: Enhancing Students' Comprehension of Text*. New York: Scholastic.

Santman, Donna. 2005. *Shades of Meaning: Comprehension and Interpretation in Middle School*. Portsmouth, NH: Heinemann.

Serafini, Frank. 2004. *Lessons in Comprehension: Explicit Instruction in Reading Workshop*. Portsmouth, NH: Heinemann.

Tovani, Cris. 2000. *I Read It, But I Don't Get It: Comprehension Strategies for Adolescent Readers*. Portland, ME: Stenhouse.

Vasquez, Vivian. 2003. *Getting Beyond "I Like the Book": Creating Space for Critical Literacy in K–6 Classrooms*. Newark, DE: International Reading Association.

Wilhelm, Jeffrey D. 2001. *Improving Comprehension with Think-Aloud Strategies: Modeling What Good Readers Do*. New York: Scholastic.

Reading and Writing Development and Assessment

In order to teach reading and writing effectively, teachers should have a solid understanding of how students develop throughout their lives as readers and writers. When I began teaching, all I really knew to do was sort students into two categories—those who could read and those who could not—based on who seemed to stay on task during independent reading. Similarly, I did not know much at all about how students develop as writers. I needed to read professional texts and engage in conversations with colleagues to begin to know the answers to the many questions I had about teaching reading and writing: What are the reading and writing behaviors and skills young readers need to develop in order to begin to learn to read and write? How do readers and writers continue to develop during elementary, middle, and high school? What do struggling readers and writers need? What assessments are useful? Knowing more about reading and writing development can help teachers determine students' strengths and areas of need and design effective lessons.

"A Call to Action: What We Know About Adolescent Literacy and Ways to Support Teachers in Meeting Students' Needs. " 2004. NCTE. May.

Allington, Richard. 2005. *What Really Matters for Struggling Readers: Designing Research-Based Programs, 2nd ed*. New York: Pearson, Allyn & Bacon.

Anderson, Carl. 2005. *Assessing Writers*. Portsmouth, NH: Heinemann.

Beers, Kylene. 2002. *When Kids Can't Read—What Teachers Can Do: A Guide for Teachers 6–12*. Portsmouth, NH: Heinemann.

Ministry of Education, ed. 1997. *Reading for Life: The Learner as Reader*. Katonah, NY: Richard C. Owen.

New Standards. 1999. *Reading and Writing Grade by Grade: Primary Literacy Standards for Kindergarten Through Third Grade*. Washington, DC: National Center on Education and the Economy.

New Standards. 2004. *Using Rubrics to Improve Student Writing*. Washington, DC: National Center on Education and the Economy. There are six books in the series, one per grade from kindergarten to fifth grade.

Sibberson, Franki, and **Karen Szymusiak.** 2003. *Still Learning to Read: Teaching Students in Grades 3–6*. Portland, ME: Stenhouse.

Szymusiak, Karen, and **Franki Sibberson.** 2001. *Beyond Leveled Books: Supporting Transitional Readers in Grades 2–5*. Portland, ME: Stenhouse.

Wilde, Sandra. 2000. *Miscue Analysis Made Easy: Building on Student Strengths*. Portsmouth, NH: Heinemann.

Instructional Approaches to the Teaching of Reading

Teachers have specific questions about what it looks like to teach reading on a day-to-day basis, such as: What are the instructional approaches teachers can use to teach students to construct meaning of texts? How do I use a read-aloud? What is reading workshop? What are the other students doing when I teach guided reading? What does shared reading look like with older students? How do literature circles work? Certainly, most of the professional texts I listed so far describe not just comprehension strategies and reading development but also how to teach students to read. But sometimes it is helpful to dive into a professional text that focuses on how to use specific instructional approaches. Here are the texts I turn to for answers about how to teach reading.

Reading Workshop

Calkins, Lucy McCormick. 2000. *The Art of Teaching Reading*. New York: Pearson, Allyn & Bacon.

Literature Circles

Daniels, Harvey. 2001. *Literature Circles: Voice and Choice in Book Clubs and Reading Groups*. Portland, ME: Stenhouse.

Daniels, Harvey, and **Nancy Steineke.** 2005. *Mini-Lessons for Literature Circles*. Portsmouth, NH: Heinemann.

Guided Reading and What the Other Students Are Doing During Guided Reading

Diller, Debbie. 2003. *Literacy Work Stations: Making Centers Work*. Portland, ME: Stenhouse.

Diller, Debbie. 2005. *Practice with Purpose: Literacy Work Stations for Grades 3–6*. Portland, ME: Stenhouse.

Fountas, Irene C., and **Gay Su Pinnell.** 1996. *Guided Reading: Good First Teaching for All Children*. Portsmouth, NH: Heinemann.

Hornsby, David. 2000. *A Closer Look at Guided Reading*. Armadale, Victoria, Australia: Eleanor Curtain. Available at www.eastmanbooks.com.

Interactive Read-Aloud

Fisher, Douglas, James Flood, Diane Lapp, and **Nancy Frey.** 2004. "Interactive Read-Alouds: Is There a Common Set of Implementation Practices?" *The Reading Teacher* 58 (1): 8–17.

Serafini, Frank, and **Cyndi Giorgis.** 2003. *Reading Aloud and Beyond: Fostering the Intellectual Life with Older Readers*. Portsmouth, NH: Heinemann.

Shared Reading

Brown, Sue. 2004. *Shared Reading for Grades 3 and Beyond: Working It Out Together*. Wellington, New Zealand: Learning Media. Available at www.pacificlearning.com.

Parkes, Brenda. 2000. *Read It Again! Revisiting Shared Reading*. Portland, ME: Stenhouse.

Content Area Reading

Daniels, Harvey, and **Steven Zemelman.** 2004. *Subjects Matter: Every Teacher's Guide to Content-Area Reading*. Portsmouth, NH: Heinemann.

Tovani, Cris. 2004. *Do I Really Have to Teach Reading? Content, Comprehension, Grades 6–12*. Portland, ME: Stenhouse.

Knowledge of Texts

On a daily basis, teachers and students make decisions about what to read. Teachers decide which texts to use as models during reading lessons, to use with students during small-group instruction, and to offer to students for consideration during literature circles and independent reading. How to match students with texts that support their reading development and how to teach students to select texts that are right for them is an ongoing issue for teachers. Teachers may ask, What makes this text more challenging than the texts my students can read already? Which texts should I use to teach my students what they need next for their learning? Your state standards may indicate that students need to be capable readers of a wide variety of types of texts like essays, process/procedural documents, short stories, traditional tales, odes, and consumer documents, some of which may be unfamiliar to your teachers. Helping teachers learn more about genres is crucial. Staying current with the titles that may interest students is also necessary. Here are some of the most useful resources I've found to help boost my knowledge of texts.

Book Links magazine, a publication of the American Library Association, which, according to their website, "provides comprehensive information for using books in the classroom, including thematic bibliographies with related discussion questions and activities, author and illustrator interviews and essays, and articles by educators on practical ways to turn children on to reading."

Fountas, Irene C., and **Gay Su Pinnell.** 1999. *Matching Books to Readers: Using Leveled Books in Guided Reading, K–3*. Portsmouth, NH: Heinemann.

Hoyt, Linda, Margaret Mooney, and **Brenda Parkes.** 2003. *Exploring Informational Texts from Theory to Practice*. Portsmouth, NH: Heinemann.

Mooney, Margaret E. 2001. *A Book Is a Present: Selecting Texts for Intentional Teaching*. Katonah, NY: Richard C. Owen.

Mooney, Margaret E. 2004. *Text Forms and Features: A Resource for Intentional Teaching*. Katonah, NY: Richard C. Owen.

Pinnell, Gay Su, and **Irene C. Fountas.** 2001. *Leveled Books for Readers Grades 3–6: A Companion Volume to Guiding Readers and Writers*. Portsmouth, NH: Heinemann. For the most current information on leveled texts, visit their website at www.fountasandpinnellleveledbooks.com/.

Young Adult Library Services Association. Lists of recommended titles available at www.ala.org/ala/yalsa/booklistsawards/booklistsbook.htm.

Instructional Approaches to the Teaching of Writing

Teachers also have many questions about how to teach writing. Some teachers need to learn more about the big picture of teaching writing such as what the writing process involves, what it means to teach students the writing process, and how to establish a writing workshop. Other teachers may have questions about specific stages of the writing process such as how to confer with students, how to teach writer's craft or revision, how to teach specific genres, and how to teach grammar, punctuation, or spelling using a workshop approach. The titles listed below span the grade levels and vary in scope to provide you with a variety of possible resources.

Writing Workshop

Atwell, Nancie. 1998. *In the Middle: New Understanding About Writing, Reading, and Learning*. Portsmouth, NH: Heinemann-Boyton/Cook.

Bomer, Randy. 1995. *Time for Meaning: Crafting Literate Lives in Middle and High School*. Portsmouth, NH: Heinemann.

Calkins, Lucy McCormick. 1994. *The Art of Teaching Writing*. Portsmouth, NH: Heinemann.

Fletcher, Ralph, and **JoAnn Portalupi.** 2001. *Writing Workshop: The Essential Guide*. Portsmouth, NH: Heinemann.

Graves, Donald H. 1994. *A Fresh Look at Writing*. Portsmouth, NH: Heinemann.

Ray, Katie Wood. 2001. *The Writing Workshop: Working Through the Hard Parts (And They're All Hard Parts)*. Urbana, IL: National Council of Teachers of English.

Conferring

Anderson, Carl. 2000. *How's It Going? A Practical Guide to Conferring with Student Writers*. Portsmouth, NH: Heinemann.

Calkins, Lucy, Amanda Hartman, and **Zoe Ryder White.** 2005. *One-to-One: The Art of Conferring with Young Writers*. Portsmouth, NH: Heinemann.

Writer's Craft and Revision

Fletcher, Ralph, and **JoAnn Portalupi.** 1998. *Craft Lessons: Teaching Writing K–8*. Portland, ME: Stenhouse.

Heard, Georgia. 2002. *The Revision Toolbox: Teaching Techniques That Work*. Portsmouth, NH: Heinemann.

Portalupi, JoAnn, and **Ralph Flectcher.** 2001. *Nonfiction Craft Lessons: Teaching Information Writing K–8*. Portland, ME: Stenhouse.

Ray, Katie Wood. 1999. *Wondrous Words: Writers and Writing in the Elementary Classroom*. Urbana, IL: National Council of Teachers of English.

Teaching Specific Genres

Angelillo, Janet. 2003. *Writing About Reading: From Book Talk to Literary Essays, Grades 3–8*. Portsmouth, NH: Heinemann.

Angelillo, Janet. 2005. *Writing to the Prompt: When Students Don't Have a Choice*. Portsmouth, NH: Heinemann.

Bomer, Katherine. 2005. *Writing a Life: Teaching Memoir to Sharpen Insight, Shape Meaning—And Triumph over Tests*. Portsmouth, NH: Heinemann.

Harvey, Stephanie. 1998. *Nonfiction Matters: Reading, Writing, and Research in Grades 3–8*. Portland, ME: Stenhouse.

Heard, Georgia. 1998. *Awakening the Heart: Exploring Poetry in Elementary and Middle School*. Portsmouth, NH: Heinemann.

Stead, Tony. 2001. *Is That a Fact? Teaching Nonfiction Writing Grades K–3*. Portland, ME: Stenhouse.

Grammar, Punctuation, and Spelling

Angelillo, Janet. 2002. *A Fresh Approach to Teaching Punctuation*. New York: Scholastic.

Ehrenworth, Mary, and **Vicki Vinton.** 2005. *The Power of Grammar: Unconventional Approaches to the Conventions of Grammar*. Portsmouth, NH: Heinemann.

Snowball, Diane, and **Faye Bolton.** 1999. *Spelling: K–8: Planning and Teaching*. Portland, ME: Stenhouse.

Teaching English Language Learners

Addressing the literacy and language needs of English Language Learners adds additional layers of complexity to our teaching. How do we teach students to read and write when English is not their native language? How do we support English language development? Here are some titles to help you and your teachers get started answering questions about teaching English Language Learners.

Cappellini, Mary. 2005. *Balancing Reading and Language Learning: A Resource for Teaching English Language Learners, K–5*. Portland, ME: Stenhouse.

Freeman, Yvonne S., and **David E. Freeman.** 2006. *Teaching Reading and Writing in Spanish and English in Bilingual and Dual Language Classrooms, Second Edition*. Portsmouth, NH: Heinemann.

Gibbons, Pauline. 1991. *Learning to Learn in a Second Language*. Portsmouth, NH: Heinemann.

Gibbons, Pauline. 2002. *Scaffolding Language, Scaffolding Learning: Teaching Second Language Learners in the Mainstream Classroom*. Portsmouth, NH: Heinemann.

 ## Reading and Writing Curriculum

One of our responsibilities as literacy coaches is to help teachers make effective decisions about curriculum design. Even teachers who are expected to follow a scope and sequence of an adopted curriculum are faced with making curriculum decisions. For example, the teachers I work with in one district realized two major issues with their adopted curriculum: first, it lacks ample instruction on reading informational texts; and second, there is far more to teach than is possible before their students take the state standards tests. The teachers read and discussed texts listed in the section Teaching Specific Genres and from the list of titles here to learn how to reorganize their mandated curriculum to better address their students' needs. Reading professional texts about short-term or long-term planning for reading and writing instruction gives teachers ideas about minilessons, assessment methods, and highly recommended texts. Plus, it helps teachers envision the bigger picture of how reading and writing units can work in concert to support literacy development. The following professional texts focus on mapping a year's worth of curriculum.

Calkins, Lucy and **The Teachers College Reading and Writing Project.** 2003. *Units of Study for Primary Writing: A Yearlong Curriculum K–2*. Portsmouth, NH: *first*hand/Heinemann.

Collins, Kathy. 2004. *Growing Readers: Units of Study in the Primary Classroom*. Portland, ME: Stenhouse.

Franzese, Rosalie. 2002. *Reading and Writing in Kindergarten: A Practical Guide*. New York: Scholastic.

Lattimer, Heather. 2003. *Thinking Through Genre: Units of Study in Reading and Writing Workshop 4–12*. Portland, ME: Stenhouse.

Ray, Katie Wood. 2002. *What You Know by Heart: How to Develop Curriculum for Your Writing Workshop*. Portsmouth, NH: Heinemann.

Ray, Katie Wood, with **Lisa Cleveland.** 2004. *About the Authors: Writing Workshop with Our Youngest Writers*. Portsmouth, NH: Heinemann.

Ruzzo, Karen, and **Mary Anne Sacco.** 2004. *Significant Studies for Second Grade: Reading and Writing Investigations for Children*. Portsmouth, NH: Heinemann.

 ## Stay Current

While building and using a robust library of professional texts is a fantastic way to continually strengthen your knowledge, I strongly encourage you to join professional organizations and subscribe to professional journals, both in print and online. When I use journal articles in professional development sessions, teachers and administrators often comment on how much they appreciate the bursts of the most current thinking the articles contain. Journals often include recommended texts for students, lesson plan ideas that can be applied immediately, suggested texts for further reading, and research that appeases the "research-based" requirement we often face.

Check out the National Council of Teachers of English at www.ncte.org. The NCTE offers journals such as *Language Arts, Voices from the Middle,* and *English Journal,* as well as publications that span all grade levels. As a sub-scriber, you can access the articles online and receive the journals in the mail. Consider subscribing to INBOX, the NCTE's weekly emailed newsletter, which contains links to news and ideas that you can use in your coaching work.

Visit the International Reading Association at www.reading.org. The IRA also offers journals such as *The Reading Teacher* and *The Journal of Adolescent and Adult Literacy* and other publications, available online or through the mail, that span all grade levels.

The National Staff Development Council at www.nsdc.org/index.cfm is rich with information that supports our work as professional development providers. Use the search engine on the site to find numerous articles about school-based staff development and other topics of interest. Also, consider subscribing to the *JSD,* which is published quarterly, or to the new electronic journal, *Teachers Teaching Teachers.*

Works Cited

Blachowicz, Camille L. Z., Connie Obrochta, and **Ellen Fogelberg.** 2005. "Literacy Coaching for Change." *Educational Leadership* 62 (6): 55–58.

Buly, Marsha Riddle, Tracy Coskie, LeAnne Robinson, and **Kathy Egawa,** eds. 2005. "From the Coaches' Corner: What Makes an Effective Literacy Coach." *Voices from the Middle* 12 (4): 60–61.

Calkins, Lucy, and **The Teachers College Reading and Writing Project.** 2003. *Units of Study for Primary Writing: A Yearlong Curriculum.* Portsmouth, NH: *first*hand/Heinemann.

Calkins, Lucy. 2000. *The Art of Teaching Reading.* Boston: Allyn & Bacon.

Cambourne, Brian. 1988. *The Whole Story: Natural Learning and the Acquisition of Literacy.* Auckland, New Zealand: Ashton Scholastic.

Cook, Lynne, and **Marilyn Friend.** 1995. "Co-teaching: Guidelines for Effective Practices." *Focus on Exceptional Children* 28 (3): 1–16.

Costa, Arthur L., and **Robert Garmston.** 2002. *Cognitive Coaching: A Foundation For Renaissance Schools.* Norwood, MA: Christopher-Gordon.

Daniels, Harvey. 2005. "The Literature Circle: Six Ways of Looking at the Achievement Gap." *Voices from the Middle* 13 (1): 58–59.

Dantonio, Marylou. 2001. *Collegial Coaching: Inquiry into the Teaching Self, Second Edition.* Bloomington, IN: Phi Delta Kappa International Inc.

Darling-Hammond, Linda. 1999. "Teacher Quality and Student Achievement: A Review of State Policy Evidence." *Education Policy Analysis Archives* 8 (1).

Darling-Hammond, Linda, and **Milbrey W. McLaughlin.** 1995. "Policies that Support Professional Development in an Era of Reform." *Phi Delta Kappan* 76 (8): 597–604.

DuFour, Richard, Robert Eaker, and **Rebecca DuFour,** eds. 2005. *On Common Ground: The Power of Professional Learning Communities.* Bloomington, IN: National Educational Service.

Fountas, Irene, and **Gay Su Pinnell.** 2000. *Guiding Readers and Writers (Grades 3–6): Teaching Comprehension, Genre, and Content Literacy.* Portsmouth, NH: Heinemann.

Fullan, Michael. 2000. *The New Meaning of Educational Change, 3rd ed.* New York: Teachers College Press.

Fullan, Michael. 2001. *Leading in a Culture of Change.* San Francisco, CA: Jossey-Bass.

Gitlin, Andrew, and **Frank Margonis.** 1995. "The Political Aspect of Reform: Teacher Resistance as Good Sense." *American Journal of Education* 103 (3): 377–405.

Greene, Terry. 2004. Literature Review for School-Based Staff Developers and Coaches. July. NCSD. www.nsdc.org/library/schoolbasedlitreview.pdf.

Hall, Barbara. 2004. "Literacy Coaches: An Evolving Role." *Carnegie Reporter* 3 (1).

Harwayne, Shelley. 1999. *Going Public: Priorities and Practice at the Manhattan New School.* Portsmouth, NH: Heinemann.

Hatch, Thomas. 2003. "The 'Long Haul' or 'Boom or Bust'? "*Education Week* 23 (2): 32–35.

Hurd, Jacqueline, and **Lori Licciardo-Musso.** 2005. "Lesson Study: Teacher-Led Professional Development in Literacy Instruction." *Language Arts* 82 (5): 388–395.

International Reading Association. 2004. *The Role and Qualifications of the Reading Coach in the United States: A Position Statement of the International Reading Association.* Newark, DE: Author.

International Reading Association. 2006. *Standards for Middle and High School Literacy Coaches.* Newark, DE: Author.

Joyce, Bruce, and **Beverly Showers.** 1988. *Student Achievement Through Staff Development, 1st ed.* New York: Longman.

Joyce, Bruce, and **Beverly Showers.** 2002. *Student Achievement Through Staff Development, 3rd ed.* Alexandria, VA: ASCD.

Knight, Jim. 2001. "FIND Strategy: Problem-Solving Process Structures in Teacher-Guided Professional Development." *Stratenotes* 2: 1–2.

Knowles, Malcolm S., Elwood F. Holton, and Richard A. Swanson. 2005. *The Adult Learner, Sixth Edition: The Definitive Classic in Adult Education and Human Resource Development*. Burlington, MA: Elsevier.

Lambert, Linda. 1998. *Building Leadership Capacity in Schools*. Alexandra, VA: ASCD. p. 3.

Lyons, Carol A., and Gay Su Pinnell. 2001. *Systems for Change in Literacy Education: A Guide to Professional Development*. Portsmouth, NH: Heinemann.

Manzo, Kathleen Kennedy. 2005. "States and Districts Send Literacy Coaches to the Rescue." *Education Week* 24 (43): 20–21.

National Staff Development Council. 2001. Standards for Staff Development. www.nsdc.org/standards/collaborationskills.cfm.

Neufeld, Barbara, and Dana Roper. June 2003. *Coaching: A Strategy for Developing Instructional Capacity Promised and Practicalities*. Cambridge, MA: Education Matters.

Pearson, P. David, and Maria Gallagher. 1983. "The Instruction of Reading Comprehension," *Contemporary Educational Psychology* 8: 22–23.

Poglinco, Susan M., Amy J. Bach, Kate Hovde, Sheila Rosenblum, Marissa Saunders, and Jonathan A. Supovitz. 2003. *The Heart of the Matter: The Coaching Model in America's Choice Schools*. Philadelphia: Consortium for Policy and Research in Education.

Robb, Laura. 2000. *Redefining Staff Development: A Collaborative Model for Teachers and Administrators* Portsmouth, NH: Heinemann.

Rock, Heidi Marie. 2002. "Job-Embedded Professional Development and Reflective Coaching." *The Instructional Leader* 5 (8): 1–4.

Sammons, Pamela. 1999. *School Effectiveness*. Lisse, The Netherlands: Swetz and Zeitlinger.

Toll, Cathy A. 2004. "Separating Coaching from Supervising." *English Leadership Quarterly* 27 (2): 5–7.

Viadero, Debra. 2000. "Lags in Minority Achievement Defy Traditional Explanations." *Education Week* 19 (28): 1, 18–22.

Vygotsky, Les S. 1962. *Thought and Language*. Cambridge, MA: MIT Press.

West, Lucy, and Fritz C. Staub. 2003. *Content-Focused Coaching: Transforming Mathematics Lessons*. Portsmouth, NH: Heinemann.

Index